SOUL RESCUE FROM SUNRISE

PETE DAWSON
ANN DAWSON

Grosvenor House
Publishing Limited

All rights reserved
Copyright © Pete Dawson & Ann Dawson, 2024

The right of Pete Dawson & Ann Dawson to be identified as the
authors of this work has been asserted in accordance with
Section 78 of the Copyright, Designs and Patents Act 1988

The book cover is copyright to Pete Dawson & Ann Dawson

This book is published by
Grosvenor House Publishing Ltd
Link House
140 The Broadway, Tolworth, Surrey, KT6 7HT.
www.grosvenorhousepublishing.co.uk

This book is sold subject to the conditions that it shall not, by way of
trade or otherwise, be lent, resold, hired out or otherwise circulated
without the author's or publisher's prior consent in any form of
binding or cover other than that in which it is published and
without a similar condition including this condition being
imposed on the subsequent purchaser.

A CIP record for this book
is available from the British Library

ISBN 978-1-83615-085-5

DEDICATED TO MY CHILDREN
DAVID & KERRY
TWO SOULS
LOST

CONTENTS

INTRODUCTION – WHERE IT ALL BEGAN		1
03-04-2015	MESSENGER	7
03-04-2015	TOM	9
29-05-2015	ABRAHAM	10
04-09-2015	ABRAHAM, ANTHONY	12
18-09-2015	ABRAHAM	15
18-12-2015	ABRAHAM	18
18-12-2015	TOOBAR	20
08-01-2016	ABRAHAM, DEREK	21
22-01-2016	ANOKU	23
05-02-2016	ABRAHAM	28
25-11-2016	JACOB	30
22-02-2019	SAMUEL	32
22-03-2019	SAMUEL, JD'S BROTHER	35
20-09-2019	WALKER	37
04-10-2019	TRIAN	40
28-10-2019	JANE	43
08-11-2019	REGGIE	48
22-11-2019	CLAIRE	53
22-11-2019	MARK & ADELE	56
13-12-2019	ADAM	57
13-12-2019	CAROL	61
03-01-2020	GODDESS AQUA, MICHAEL	63

07-01-2020	GODDESS AQUA	65
07-02-2020	GODDESS AQUA	66
06-03-2020	GODDESS AQUA	68
06-03-2020	GILL'S SISTER	69
24-04-2020	GODDESS AQUA, JAMES	72
08-05-2020	GODDESS AQUA, KARL SCHNEIDER, STACEY GOLDBERG	75
22-05-2020	GODDESS AQUA, JACOB	80
19-06-2020	GODDESS AQUA, ABDUL	83
03-07-2020	GODDESS AQUA, RICHARD Re: RACHEL	86
14-08-2020	ARGOS	90
25-09-2020	SAMANTHA, EWAN McGREGOR	93
05-02-2021	ANTHONY	95
05-03-2021	NICOLA	98
19-03-2021	NO-ONE SPECIAL BORN IN HUDDERSFIELD	99
16-04-2021	FRANCIS	101
14-05-2021	GORDON	106
11-06-2021	IDA	109
25-06-2021	HILDA	112
30-07-2021	LOUISE	115
13-08-2021	JOAN	120
10-12-2021	BARRY Re: BARBARA	125
07-01-2022	ABIGAIL	129

21-01-2022	RAYMOND	132
18-03-2022	ANOKU, AXL	137
01-04-2022	ANOKU, JUKA	141
20-05-2022	ANOKU, JACOB	145
03-06-2022	STELLA	150
08-07-2022	MESSENGER	155
19-08-2022	MESSENGER	158
02-09-2022	PEGGY Re: LOU	163
16-09-2022	WATER RUNS DEEP	169
19-09-2022	CISSY, JANICE	173
14-10-2022	ANGELINA	179
GLASTONBURY CALLING		185
ACKNOWLEDGEMENTS		194

INTRODUCTION – WHERE IT ALL BEGAN

Who would have believed it? Certainly not me! A working-class kid, the fourth of eight children, talking to SPIRITS... channelling spirits from another realm! Spirits who want their story told, some ordinary lives, some extraordinary lives, and some from worlds you just wouldn't believe! Extra-terrestrial lives – yes, even spirit from other worlds, other realms, want their stories told.

I am an ordinary chap – Pete – from an ordinary family, with an extraordinary story to tell!

I was always a very sensitive child. My early memories were visits in the middle of the night, of faces glaring at me in the darkness! I would hide under the blankets and yell, 'Go away, go away,' much to the annoyance of my siblings. As I grew, the images of the faces became much less frequent.

I was 20 years old when, out of the blue, my father passed away. For years he had suffered with bronchitis, and I can still recall his incessant coughing. The night after he passed, I awoke to hear my father cough, cough, coughing, my little sister Susan was also woken by dad's coughing, so we were both extremely spooked by this, to say the least.

The following night, I woke again... to see my father standing at the bottom of my bed. He smiled at me then waved goodbye as he slowly faded away.

By the age of twenty-one, I was married and family life began. My life was extremely busy, but something was stirring within me and I didn't quite understand what this was. It led me on a quest, searching for something, but I really didn't understand what at all I was searching for.

Many, many years later, I found myself divorced and living alone. I would often spend time with my brother Keith, who was always a lively companion! It was whilst visiting my brother one evening that I became intrigued by one of his neighbours, or rather by what she was up to late into the evening hours. Keith and I had been out for a few beers and as I was leaving him just past midnight, his neighbour Barbara was returning home. Being rather inquisitive, I asked her what she had been up to. To which my brother playfully replied, 'She's been to a spooky night!'

I was intrigued and began asking Barbara questions, becoming enthralled by what she was telling me. Consequently, she invited me to the next so-called 'Development Circle', run by her friend and colleague Wynn. I readily accepted, but little did I know that my introduction into the circle found me a lone male sitting in a circle, late into the evening, with seven females!

At the time, I did not comprehend that this circle was the beginning of my spiritual journey. More importantly, it is where I met the true love of my life, my soulmate Ann and together our spiritual journey began.

I attended the development circle for almost two years. It was where I felt comfortable, confident, and where I grew to understand that the nuisance of my childhood was in fact reality – a place where death meets life and life meets death. It is as ordinary as walking into the kitchen and turning on your tap for a glass of water.

I had no fear, only excitement and reverence for this ordinary kid from an ordinary family with an extraordinary gift of being able to communicate with people who were actually dead!

As time moved on I joined the SNU (Spiritualist National Union), and for the following fourteen years Ann & I helped to run a Spiritualist church in our local area, along with a development circle.

One day during 2012, whilst channelling spirit, I was instructed by spirit to set up a 'Trance Circle'. It would be a closed circle, and I was told exactly who to invite to sit with me in this circle – seven individuals, all healers. I was told that the whole purpose of the circle was for 'Soul Rescue' – to support lost or trapped souls who, having left their mortal body, were reluctant or found it impossible to move forward into the spirit realm.

On one particular occasion, Ann and I were told by spirit that we were on the Rainbow Path and we must go up north as soon as possible because there was a lady that would be able to help us. Intrigued by this, Ann immediately booked a coach trip to Whitby. Why Whitby? Simply, it was the only available coach trip heading up to the north of the country that week.

We stayed at the Royal Hotel, where a lady who happened to be sitting on our dining table each day introduced herself as Anita. Anita informed us that she had been told by spirit that someone needed her help and that she was aware that it was me. She informed us that this trip to Whitby had by no means been planned by herself; in fact, she had been planning a trip to Scotland. But it seems that spirit intervened and Whitby had become her new destination.

Anita was indeed a spiritual leader, based at Lytham, St Anne's near Blackpool. We learned that she was a spirit channeler, soul reader, and healer. It was Anita who confirmed what I already knew to be true, an understanding and a knowing that our innermost feelings from deep within our soul begin to stir from the minute we are born.

Often, we know we have walked this path before, but each time we must learn many lessons. We may come to realise the meaning for finding ourselves back on this earth at this particular time. We may have had stirrings within, which make our soul troubled. But whenever man is troubled, he only has to turn to God for help, many do not do this. Instead, they turn to other material means, but this may often be only a temporary solution as it never leads one back to the root cause. For example, if a tree is dying, you may have to look at the roots or leaves to establish the reason why. The leaves represent oneself; the roots are our soul.

We discovered that the Rainbow path is the path of healing – healing the spirit within. God promised the rainbow in the sky, after the rain, making all things new. It is not an easy path; it needs discipline and along with that, inner strength.

In these times we sometimes lack the discipline to meditate. However, perseverance would enable us to find the peace that is always present within our heart centre. We do forget why we are here and the many lessons waiting for us to learn, but it is all part of the bigger picture.

The wonderful colours of the rainbow draw you towards it, as does the sun and its warm healing rays. The light will guide you into an age of love, light and healing, not only healing for ourselves, but also for our wonderful planet that is, as we all know, crying out for love and care.

Just a note before you begin this journey. The following excerpts are words from direct communication with spirit, channelled by myself at our fortnightly trance circle held at our home 'Sunrise' in Worcestershire. Over a period of many years I was instructed by my spirit guide that the purpose of the circle is twofold: To open a channel for lost souls to find their way back to the light, to return home; and to balance planet earth's energies.

I have included a selection that I think you may find interesting and certainly thought-provoking. The english written word and grammar in the following excerpts is far from exceptional, but to retain the authenticity of the words spoken by spirit, the text has not been revised. It has passed through the filter of my mind and voice box, and therefore is written as spoken, undoctored.

May you be guided to take from it what you need at any particular point in time.

The hearts on the back cover have great significance within our story. One of the first hearts was a gift from Anthony – one of the rescued souls who passed through the channel. This heart was given to us in gratitude for our help with his journey. He asked for a hand-carved beechwood heart to be placed in the centre of our circle with his name carved on the top of it. Anthony was a US marine fighting the Japanese in the Pacific Ocean during WW2. His home was Welcome, a small town in Louisiana, USA. There are many souls who have also asked for their names to be placed on the beechwood hearts over the years in gratitude. You will learn a little more about some of them as the story unfolds.

This is just a little background to help you to begin to understand my extraordinary journey. I do hope you enjoy and are amazed by the incredible stories of lives lived, lives lost and the memories and insights these souls have so graciously shared with us all.

03-04-2015   MESSENGER

Greetings, it is I Messenger.

Scientists of your world now observe the spider, what information it can give. The spider spins its web for food and waits as the snake waits for its prey. Man, for one of your phrases, runs around like a headless chicken, in search of its destiny and its future; what lies ahead? So much can be learned from the humble spider.

There are great temples around your world, many religions – Christianity is just one. As your world evolves, many religions inter-marry. A child from those marriages has choice, but the child has harsh lessons to learn.

We have spoken of this before. Those in your world that are talented, you give them a knighthood, why? They come to your world to fulfil a purpose; to fulfil that purpose will move them on in our world, to move onto another task and another and another. If that task is not fulfilled, they will come back to do it all again.

It is not easy for the human body; so many limitations. The soul is not in charge of the body. It is an observer, to learn, to observe, not control.

As your world speeds up, so too does mental capacity. If the mental capacity takes no more, therefore the blueprint will change. The soul does not come to your world with restrictions; it comes to observe and learn. The one great thing the soul learns is patience.

To travel is so mundane, so slow. To put into simple terms for you, your world is like a bird in a gigantic cage. Open the door and the bird is free to go in any direction it wishes, no restrictions. Yes, you have your dwelling, your home you call your base. You may move from one to another, but it is your home, all that is familiar to you. In our world we have many homes in many countries; yes, a family in each country. To come to your world – what you would call a dry run – the soul is not thrust into a body without knowledge of your world. To visit, yes, to see the atrocities and the hatred. Love in our world is supreme. It would be naive to send a soul to earth unprepared.

If we talk of our life as an onion, we peel a layer and then another, and so it goes on, each layer is uncovered. The rings on a tree, when it is cut – each ring is growth, each ring is knowledge. The rising of the seas, the changing of your world, the advancement of scientists and engineers. We have spoken before of the speed your world catches up with other worlds.

We hear talk of humans living for five hundred years, we smile. We have said two hundred of your years, stretching like an elastic band a little. Many, many diseases will be eradicated, but not all. It is not an accident you have all come together, not an accident you are all healers. The lives have been together before – male, female, it makes no difference. There are those of you whose lives were secret. Those of you, shall we say, who had their physical lives taken away.

Farewell for now.

03-04-2015 TOM

I moved to New Zealand with my beloved Beth and daughter Sasha. As I child, I would read her nursery rhymes to help her develop, to teach the mind and develop the love and the bond of a child to the parent.

In your world, accountancy was my profession. I worked long hours, looking forward to retirement, but it was not to be.

The soul runs along parallel lines, for the soul to enter the human body, not unlike a child. The human body is the parent for that soul to learn and develop – in an ideal world the soul – until natural death, when the human body would close down of old age. We do not have control when a person takes their own life.

If disease ravages the body and the body decays, it teaches so much to the soul. If your body is snatched away from the soul, in your world you have convalescing. It is said there are hospitals in our world, but they are what is known as restings, where the soul can adjust – only for those who are snatched without warning, I have suffered the latter. My beloved Beth taken away in the winter chill of 1964.

The scientists of your world and astronomers will make a breakthrough, Neptune and Uranus. There will be knowledge also of another world.

For now farewell.

29-05-2015   ABRAHAM

We do understand the dilemmas you go through. We try to make you understand. When we give you insight, it is not meant to come across as dour. We spoke of scientists. It is the duty of mankind to live a human life, a natural law. Each solar system lives, works pure, to rid the body of disease, of all species, to prolong life. We have spoken of cancers, Hodgkinson's disease, MS and heart attacks, so easy to fix.

The longer you live, the more knowledge you will bring back with you. Strains of bacteria will be produced and inserted into the body to kill diseased cells and promote healthy cells. Others will come to earth to find cures. News will come regularly, optimism for every breakthrough. The natural resources of your world are being drained. Artificial supplements will become necessary. Your world will become reliant on scientists who work in laboratories.

Natural resources of your earth, plates buckle, the effect on your world will be a little way off as yet. Earth will bake, freeze and flood. The dramatic change of your buildings will also take effect. No buildings will be higher than three storeys. Landscape and architecture will change. Rubber and a new plastic for replacement organs. Buildings will be made that way, too, for safety. Your earth will be sustainable.

You all have choices to return. As you have been told before, your choice is limitless. To stay in spirit or return to earth, or to other worlds; you have a choice. Do not be naïve to think you have only lived on earth, for you have many homes.

The spider's web is not unbelievable. For those on earth fleeing one country to another is meant, for other cultures to mix as one. Does not knowledge entwine? We have said choice; those who stay on earth are taken as lost souls, it is not so. Earth's energies are a greater pull for them. It is their choice to work, as others in other worlds.

We hear you speak of the magpies being destructive. Look at it from a different point of view. The robin builds its nest. To steal one's home you say from another, you say is the devil's work. One to toil for another to snatch away is not the devil's work, but clever? For the robin to build another, for the magpie to steal, so it goes on. If man built a home to have it later stolen, in time you would say man is foolish. The magpie would have an empire of homes and nests – one rich, one poor. Would robin or man learn a lesson, to build a nest that cannot be stolen, for man to build his home, his castle impregnable? Lessons to be learnt.

We see an influx of life returning to our world. Natural disasters are rife, lives lost, those that travel by train, lives lost at sea, flooding of islands. In your year of 2015, we light a candle for each one of you. A flame burns brightly.

I bid you farewell.

04-09-2015   ABRAHAM, ANTHONY

It is I, Anthony.

I have been given permission to speak. I will not take up too much of your time. We were called out to the Twin Towers. The scale that met us is something that we just can't describe to you. I loved my job; I was proud to serve; it was a mixture of adrenalin, fear, and the privilege of serving.

The thought always went through our minds, for our colleagues, our friends, if ever we moved bodies burned and charred. For there were those of us with no body to find. One moment it was dark, then like a light had been switched on, it was brilliant... Confusion, where was I?

It pleases me to see my wife has moved on, and my beautiful daughter who has a daughter herself now, with beautiful blue eyes just like hers.

What I have come to say to you: 'We bear no grudges for those who hijack planes, for in our world revenge and hate is not an emotion. Those emotions are bred in your world and others. It is easy to say but hard to digest. These are the teachings of the Nazarene – odd but true, like serving an apprenticeship.

Thank you for listening to me.

ABRAHAM

Good evening, friends, and welcome.

Tonight, I would like to talk to you about the frail and the elderly. There are those who wear a crude device you call a panic button. In time we will call it a microchip; this will be embedded in the arm of the elderly. If a person was to collapse, it would trigger an alarm in a database. It will tell them if a person is experiencing heart failure, stroke, etc. It will tell them exactly where they are – for example, at home, shops, etc. This is just a minor advancement in your world. Age concern for the elderly, the treatment they receive, the technical advancement. In just two of your years, what is modern will become antiquated. That is the speed of technology.

The demands on your world, the heavy strain put on your food supplies, again scientists have no choice but for food to come in tablet form to be stored for many years. But this is light years away in your world. It will become the norm and accepted.

We talk about the woodpigeon, for we know the badger carries disease, the woodpigeon also. This will cause great concern, contamination of soil, land will be burnt. There will also be a new threat – hurricanes.

The time will come when people will be frightened to leave their homes; there will be safety in numbers. This is the darkness that will prevail in your world.

Temporary though it is, it will happen. You will not see this in your lifetime, but again you have choice.

I have spoken before of the sun disappearing in your world. On its return, it will be extreme, the world will bake. These extreme conditions will become normal – on a temporary basis but for many years – to work in darkness. Many will live amongst the stars, and parties will return to earth to give updates to see if your earth is habitable again. It makes us sad in our world. Many times awareness comes, but it is only temporary. Disaster strikes your earth in many ways. Soon, the return to normality – or what you may call normality.

An insight we give you, awareness, call it a balance, there are times you will bring back memories and times you will not.

I will leave you with one thought: Your time on this earth is a blink of an eye.

God's blessings on you all.

18-09-2015   ABRAHAM

We talk of a cure for Parkinson's, Hodgkin's disease, bipolar, and brain cancer, to mention a few. Scientists coming together with a medical team, there will be breakthrough after breakthrough. More discoveries all the time as your world advances and there is a serum being worked on at this present time which will reduce tumours of the brain by more than 50%.

Surgery will not be as you think of it, scalpels will be a thing of the past; laser is the way forward, limiting the size of the tumour. Laser treatment reduces the risk of veins and blood vessels being damaged. So much in your world that is primitive and archaic.

There has been much publicised of robots. The intelligence of robot models is so primitive. The youngsters of today will develop machines that look human, bodily smells of humans, elastic-aged skin, the touch and feel of humans. There will be breakthrough after breakthrough as scientists and medical teams catch up fast on your world. Polished stainless steel will be used in the body; it will become the norm. You now have replacement hips, knees, and shoulders, but every joint in the human anatomy there will be a replacement for. For in time – many, many moons away – if a limb is damaged beyond repair and removed by laser, technology will allow regrowth of that limb.

What we give you at these meetings is an insight into the future of your world. We understand the knowledge and the things we say, a natural reaction would be:

I don't want to be around at that time. A natural process changes everything; a world you are born into is natural and normal.

In time, stainless steel will be what you call old hat. There are those of you that will say it is against nature. Is it not natural to advance in your world? To progress to evolve the circle is never-ending. The circle is sacred in our world; there is no break, no split. Your earthly sun is round and your moon is round, planets that you know of in your solar system are also round. If you split a circle and turn it horizontal, it will resemble an arch. An arch has great strength.

God created a planet where life will thrive. Evolution is never-ending, the circle of life. Your Earth holds many secrets, many discoveries, not only what we call spiritual sites, wastelands and buildings that are demolished and ground excavated. There are many riches and treasures that come in scientific form. Man must learn that knowledge, and it should be used in the correct manner. For man uses power to destroy, but nature will respond.

We watch carefully the mass migration of countries, the feeble efforts of man with wire fences; they treat those like wild animals with such despair. The leaders of your world, a radical, radical shakeup is required; your solar system, other planets have been found. The link with discoveries found on your earth. This will be proven life outside your solar system; this is just one knowledge.

There are therapies used in your world – an alternative medicine. Hypnosis will become widely recognised with paranoia and schizophrenia. Those gifted to take mankind back in their minds, places where their subconscious will not allow. The benefits of the therapy will be widely used, and there won't be as much scepticism. For the resources you use with your brain currently account for only one-third of your brain capacity. The children not yet born, the capacity of their brain will be greater. This will be a gradual process, allowing your world to catch up. Those roots will grow; spiritualism will become the norm.

We do not say the voice box will become primitive and not used, but thought will become the communication, there will be choice. Touching and embracing will always be, for the touching of bodies embracing each other, you say the feel-good factor, it cannot be replaced. Laughter is an antidote, physical embrace is an antidote, emotions will always remain.

Do not despair all developments of the human brain. All thoughts will not be read, privacy of the mind is paramount to each individual.

We would look forward to your next meeting to make you understand your purpose on this earth.

Farewell, my friends.

18-12-2015   ABRAHAM

Think of your world in nature, the size of a marble to the human eye. Look down on your planet and you would see the four corners of your world in one. My purpose was to give you a clear indication to your world. You do not see the country and the continents, for each of your countries speak in a different tongue. There is no barrier, for we all speak in the native tongue.

Time will come when disease will not be fought with medicine; the brain will fight disease. The idea part of the brain allows disease to grow throughout the human body. In time you will be able to fight disease with the power of your mind, your brain capacity. It will not be a struggle in the future to fight disease.

What you call Spiritualism is a new religion on your earth. In time, many, many moons away, this will be the main religion. Communication from one world to another will be telepathic; thought will become universal. Advancement will be gradual. For the thought of another world, to make you understand would blow fuses in your brain. Advancement will be slow. The advancement of the human brain is beyond your comprehension. To play music that you dance to, does not that music control your mind? Think of it what you will – a song, a musical drama. If you think of your time as a musical drama or a pantomime, there is somewhere in between where you play to the tune. That is the purpose of your lives each day. Some of you hit a dud note, for that is when you learn the most.

The element of free will is to be utilised, another to talk now.

Respect to you all.

18-12-2015   TOOBAR

My name is Toobar; my father was Juan, as a small baby, he took me to the great river. As an infant, time would be spent among the coral, learning to fish. Before the age of three of your years I was an established fisher boy. At six of your years, I was left alone to fish daily. At the age before puberty, I went with the elders to hunt, trap and snare.

Before my late teenage years, the Spanish came. I was taken in the night into the belly of a great boat. I was one of the lucky ones – I did not reach land, death became me. Fish ate my flesh, this pleased me to give back to them what they gave to me.

My sister Akter was not a lucky woman. She worked the crops, she had four children and later died of disease.

Farewell.

08-01-2016   ABRAHAM, DEREK

It is I, Abraham, Lord of the mountains. It does not matter how you welcome – to sit is all that is required of you. It matters not if you worship Allah, Buddha, or Christ worship is worship it is the intent that counts. Let me tell you, Jerusalem will not fall; it will remain in the heart and soul. We did foretell of the collapse of China. Look to the country you call Russia – the younger generation will say no. The leaders of your countries in your world are like pawns, a game of chess trying to outdo each other. Greed at the highest level. We tell you time and time again, greed will be the undoing of your world.

Friends, we have spoken of the great libraries, there are concerts, music, great operas, pop, and sports arenas. Sport is very powerful in our world, and yes, there are those from our world who live amongst you. Reports, dossiers, hidden, so much information. No matter how deep the vaults, they can be opened and truth will prevail. Strides that man will make, it is unclear at this present time. It will be thought of as the greatest moment in mankind, which is what you will call space stations. To shuttle those with wealth, from earth, a small advancement for mankind.

I will allow another to speak with you very briefly.

DEREK

I apologise to break up your meeting, my name is Derek, my time on earth was not a pleasant time. I was what you would call a 'mummy's boy', bullied at school, and what you would call a loner. I took my own life. When you take your own life, you do not go to the lower level. It is not a crime to take your own life. It was my life I took, not another's.

There is much counselling, much comfort, for those who take their own lives, from those who also have taken their own lives before them. No-one can understand unless they have been there themselves. The adjustment and rehabilitation can be very lengthy. Let me tell you, those ascend one step only from the lower level; they have to adjust.

On the earth, it is like being shackled in chains from head to foot, so much to learn. I do apologise again, I was always told to stop saying sorry. Stop and think before you speak to another harshly, try putting them first before yourself. Words become trapped inside the body, where they fester and fester. Please, please, heed these words.

Thank you for listening to me.

22-01-2016   ANOKU

We have spoken many times of this human body and mind. Let me tell you of the evolution and changes to your planet. The human will change and adapt. Water will become second nature to you. Great vessels – what you call ocean liners – they will be miniature in size as to what will come. A new plastic will replace metal, a density so robust; great vessels that carry machines, such will be the magnitude of those vessels. They will also launch vessels into your space. Mankind will live on those vessels for many years. Professors, scientists in great laboratories.

The stars you can see with the human eye in your galaxy and those that reach far beyond the human eye in what you call space centres. Great magnification you cannot view, twin earths far far beyond in the great galaxies of life. In time, man, scientists and engineers will develop technology, breakthrough after breakthrough. The stargate another word circulating around your world – would you not call where you sit this day and record the channel and the prayer of Lady Ann, the exodus of those souls began? Search your minds, scratching away a great mine (Mark opened this channel). It was like scratching a mine with a nail file, such achievements not to be scoffed at.

Is this channel not a stargate? Each world has many stargates, stars in your galaxy minor and major planets. Mass exodus of your world – there is truth, although a little twisted. Would that exodus be caused by nature, mankind, or will that exodus be of craft, manmade, or both? There is a fable in your world, Noah's ark, and a great wooden ship, also the floods. It has been said great ships will travel your skies deep into your galaxy. The young the healthy and the rich, others will follow and the elderly will not be forgotten.

Let's talk of earth angels, they travel your earth, they walk amongst you unnoticed 99% of the time. Talk of miracles on your earth, they play their part.

The sun is of great importance, but again the sun is mirrored. This is to allow for that great escape. Would this be the reason each world mirrors itself? Why would earth be the only priority? Life is precious in bodily form for all species, all worlds. Each individual serves for one common cause, to put glory on that cause. You can call it the golden age – a label only. Look beyond a label, no matter how grand it may appear.

I am aware of the confusion of the time that I speak. I will talk on one matter again with permission from Jacob. Yes, I avoided; you would call it skirting around. Without permission from Jacob, I would not say. I was one of the perpetrators for the loss of Jacob's beloved. Jacob at that time was so full of hate, he moved at stealth under the cover of darkness, he lay low when the sun was full. Titus was the first to be slain. There were suspicions, but not until the second perpetrator was slain.

Jacob left his calling card – an arrow above the knee to render helpless. The tour began, both bodies identical leaving no doubt. I, Anoku, was guarded day and night, full of remorse and full of guilt. I made my escape under cover of darkness. Evening, those guards, I walked towards the great sands. I wore flimsy clothing in the knowledge if Jacob didn't find me, I would freeze. So, death was guaranteed. On entering the great sands, the wild cries were deafening. In the distance the creatures of the sands cries rang out into the night. Little did I know they were warning Jacob of danger. The call soon started to take its effect as my walk became slower and slower. In the distance, through blurred eyesight, a figure stood with bow arched. Jacob, I come to you, to take my life. There was hesitation before that arrow struck accurately to the heart centre, death was instant, peace was overwhelming. On my return, I could not penetrate the dark. The guilt and remorse remained, a question repeated over and over again whilst in that dark: Jacob, why did you not give me the death I deserved?

It has been said many times, there is no existence of time in our world. Let me tell you, the dark was a life sentence. Only when the dark became lighter still, a low level, the figure stood in front of me. He had been allowed to descend from level one. You gave yourself up willingly. I felt in that moment your guilt and remorse; it became automatic to offer my arm. 'Anoku,' he said, 'you are not like the others, you learnt forgiveness before your return, you also learnt forgiveness before I.' Then he was no longer there. Not until many challenges and level five did we greet each other. Respect for each other, for respect and love is in our world. (Anoku was one of three who killed Jacob's wife when they lived on another world.)

There is a saying in your world: one soul, many lives. Choice is always there. A soul may enter a body and return when that body dies. The soul may remain or return again and again to whichever world. We will use earth as an example. One soul may return and return; another soul may return to a different world. It is a fable, not written, a soul returns again and again. You are all intelligent people it does not take much understanding. If you return, you return with a blank canvas. To return knowing of a previous life would be like walking through treacle. On our world you know of each life – that is preparation, great knowledge, great learning, of each life. There are those on our world who would never enter a body. Put a name on them if you wish, call them angels, helpers of the source. So, each time you return you know of each life, the essence of that life remains.

Where is that home? The great facet? It is not coincidence. Those that cross your path have crossed your path before. The facet is great and each family is great, for those strands hold us all together. So do we understand when someone crosses your path and you feel you know them from before. The subconscious recognises that strand. So, for all of you, have no fear, the essence of each life remains. The contact is your choice, there are those you wish to meet and those you don't respect. Again, it is always a choice and love is always.

I, Anoku, and Jacob have climbed great mountains to become pure and full of love. Your mountains will be small hilltops only. For one of you who sits today, the ground is level and the wind blows and their kite flies high in the wind. A new energy will join on our next visit. I will not say this is my last visit; I leave that gateway open. Let it be known, the privilege to serve, not only to serve, for I have gained great knowledge from you.

Mankind, unforeseen knowledge changes the landscape of your earth. Knowledge in the wrong hands has great danger. Knowledge also brings great rewards but can also be man's downfall, man has so much to learn. Transparency will come.

My blessings, from the great source, the essence of you all. That door will remain open, if I am granted.

Au Revoir my friends.

05-02-2016   ABRAHAM

We spoke on our last visit of great ships to be built on your world, built for durability and strength. A steel skeleton, steel yet to be fabricated, in your world. A plastic body so dense, so strong, durable, and flexible at the same time.

The dreams of mankind, homes will be built on similar lines, for your homes, your dwellings, now the material is so brittle it will crack. Dwellings built to withstand an earthquake on your earth. The human structure of bone surrounded with a principal body. Dwellings with sensors for when the rain falls and the floods come. They will rise automatically with a built-in warning system, untold amount of lives saved by such simple methods.

The poor countries of your world where disease is rife, the affluent of your world cause disease. Pollution will kill off the vulnerable, birds will fall from your skies, insects will perish in toxic soil.

Electric machines will be the future for a little while, then an inner energy will be found. Other worlds observe the outdated way that you live, but your world will catch up quick. In your terms you will go from a cart horse to a greyhound at great speed, stage by stage the changes will advance.

Let me tell you, children born with a small skull, an antidote will be found sooner than later. Scientists will go into overdrive, professors will work together in laboratories to find a serum that will eradicate disease. We have told you before, with your own brain so slow to appreciate the intricate working of your own brain.

Yes, your world is very harsh, the dedication of your candle, those thoughts go out into the cosmos. Harsh realities of your world are meant, the moment you are conceived. In our world you will see how futile harshness is; the reality is that at the present time you are not in our world.

So much data goes back, records on the way you live, the strides you have made with telephone companies, the mobile phone is still primitive. The mouthpiece attached you call the landline will advance, too. It will not just ring, but there will be the face of the communicator. You have what you call Skype; it will be in a similar vein. Thoughts, to transport to your loved one, far away but it will come. We do not criticise but we point out to you.

Let me tell you, it is an honour to serve. It is our privilege to be with you, not vice versa.

Farewell.

25-11-2016   JACOB

Welcome followers, it is I, Jacob. The hours of dark movement travel. I will explain to you the great sands when the wind blows, a pleasure to me. To move under cover of darkness and to rest during the day. The winds blow, the sands give me breathing space from my enemies. The great sands my home for many years, a legend to folk, many talk of Jacob never to be found. A choice I did not have, for revenge taken.

I took great care for my little girl Miranda, my daughter. Under cover of darkness, we travelled to a village far, far away where she grew up. I am biased, a fair-haired beauty, for I would gaze on her from afar, never to endanger her life. From that night she did not set eyes on me again, but I watched her grow and become a mother.

The great sands, my home to travel, to feed, to sleep by day, for I was too clever to be found. But a lonely, lonely life. I was happy in the knowledge Miranda was well loved. Revenge for torture of my love stolen from me. A weakness, turn the other cheek and a love I understand from our world (spirit world) on your world there are those in the minority.

I look forward to the seasons on your world. Autumn shows a slight resemblance to our world, tree leaves turn gold and deep brown; our world is full of colour. If it is your wish, as it is mine to live in the sands, your wish is your little oasis, it is your dream. It matters not if loved ones have a different oasis to you, for in our world there are no barriers.

When Master Peter sleeps, I travel your world, conspiracy secrets locked away, even from the most powerful men on the planet, they do not know hidden agendas. I know that Abraham has spoken of scientists, engineers, blueprints, sophisticated machines bolted to the oceans of your world, where currents flow with electricity. We foresee the future of your world, the rock at the bottom of the ocean, foundation and protection. There are homes to be built, laboratories to be fed by machines. Laboratories... yes, in the depths of your ocean, fed by electricity.

Countries of your world plot assassinations of those in power, the infighting in your world intrigues me. The object of life, the primal instinct of all life is to survive. To move on or to stay... many will choose another life.

Throughout time, man quickly adapted and greed took over. It remains deep rooted, for some it is never enough. Sophistication of weapons in your world are a threat to modern civilisation. You will see the changes that will come, a wild beast in the night, circumstances can be tamed.

Other life forms found on this earth, buried files. Naples is a pinpoint for other worlds. Resources will penetrate Naples and spread love veins across your world. There is no need to fret, no danger, collecting data as they go. Data will have riches for their worlds, they respond but the fine tuning, the instruments are far too dated on your earth.

A hand of a loved one closest to you in our world, the hand on your shoulders, the hand to bring peace to your mind and to your soul. I bid you farewell.

22-02-2019 SAMUEL

Good afternoon, Samuel here, as those before me, Abraham and Jacob.

Let me tell you a little of my life I have already started. My father was British, my mother Persian. Educated in India, my father was a high-flyer, high finance to consult companies, where to invest. This would take him away from the family home. My education, top schools as my brother JD, top qualifications. My father chose the university, much to my dismay, I declined. The anger boiled inside him: 'I worked so hard for both of you, the best education to give you a start in life.' I tried to explain to him that he was never there! I wanted a father to be a father to me.

I had a natural gift for sales. I floated from one job to another. One fortunate day in the market town, I noticed a mother and daughter, textiles so finely woven, intricate patterns, the skill was so obvious. I was very frugal with money; what savings I had, I bought a small shop. I posed the question to the mother and daughter: 'If I find you orders, will you work for me?' There was scepticism but slowly and surely the orders flowed, skilled workers came in. It was not for me to interview them; what did I know of such things? I had a natural talent for business, and unlike my father I limited the size of our business, exports grew. To learn one lesson, to be a family man, my beautiful daughter, do I need to tell you the mother?

The young girl that worked on the market with her mother, the best day of my life. My daughter was a free spirit, the love of plants and a fascination with the leaves, not once did I interfere. Great pride in my daughter, she has no wish to follow me. She is now a Professor of Biology, surprise her grandfather spent most of his working life! America is where she resides now.

Such a contrast to Jacob, whose life was torn apart, I count myself fortunate for a loving wife and daughter to control a business that doesn't take over your life. There are two ends of the spectrum with Jacob, and one thing important for you all to remember is to be grateful for the love you have received and the love you still receive, for that is the greatest gift of all.

In our world you will come to understand the meaning of love. You may think you understand now, but you have only scratched the surface. There are pockets in our world, you may call them towns, you may call them cities. You will find your own town; imagine your home and it will be there. To travel in our world, just think it and you are there. Rest assured your loved ones are at peace, they enjoy each other's company, it is not all service. Why not have idle chat? It is understandable that you want to hear of wonderful things, the masters, the grand masters, the importance.

My beautiful wife, Meesha, was taken from me – a curse you would call cancer. Angelina did show her strength; she became a woman the day her mother died. Angelina was the angel from God.

My background brings different qualities of Jacob's understanding of your earth. It is human nature to ask questions; it is the norm. On my next visit I have been given permission for each of you to ask a question.

Farewell for now.

22-03-2019   SAMUEL, JD'S BROTHER

This moment is precious for me; this is my first group, no supervision. This will bring fond memories for me. My time will come when I travel from group to group, earthly matters for all to learn. My brother JD, in high finance like my father. The pride he felt for his son and dismay for his other son, but what price did JD pay? He did not learn from our father. A broken marriage and divorce, two sons that would never speak to him. Yes, he had security but in retirement a lonely man. Family is so important.

The only time my father paid interest in me was with our business. He tried to interfere; in no uncertain terms I made it clear to him to stay away. My daughter Angelina, my free spirit, I would never interfere. She loved her grandfather. My father would bring her plants from his travels, which she adored. A bond, the only time I saw a human side. Why do I tell you of this? There are those of you here who have family rifts. To be loving, no matter what comes back in return. Human nature, what is so important? I understand when you come to our world you will wonder why all those things so important – the working life, finance, security. On your return to our world you will come to realise earth is a life of fantasy. The human mind so programmed, touch one emotion and explode another. How can you imagine a life without a human body, human mind taken away? To live a life of beauty and love, serenity is a golden world.

A slight insight, what is God? What form do you give God? An energy, an orb so brilliant, think of God as an I – all follow God and all are full of God light. If you pass an exam, you go onto the next level, and so on. You have to be worthy, qualities you bring with you. Ascended masters always aim higher.

Farewell.

20-09-2019   WALKER

Hello, I am Walker.

I am not alone, as there is a high energy with me. I am what you would say 'on parole', don't be confused I am from the dark; there is a dark in our world for those who take a human life.

Born in New York, my father was a printer, a hardworking, decent man; my mother very, very loving, as was my sister Claire. Love was alien to me. 'Mother, do not hug me.' She would despair, 'Why do I have a child who is this way?' Brought up in a very tough area, which fitted me like a glove. My father had the idea to harness my aggression, to teach me to box. Very soon I was fighting bigger and heavier. They lacked what I had, the instinct I was born with to destroy.

In my late teens I would earn far more than my father. Work as a debt collector, no payment the result a beating, again no payment, and a more severe beating. I was to progress to firearms, firearms became so natural to me I was what you call a 'hit man'. Again, what you would call the Mafia, they would hire me. I would work for them, not with them, it was just a job. My father would work each day as a printer. My job was to take life, no emotion, a job which I took seriously. So why am I here? Before my return, a family a wife a son and a daughter. The love did not change; they were there, an irritant at times. Their lives cut short, it was said it was payback time, an excuse to slaughter. Let me tell you, there is always one faster and better.

On my return I was aware of lying on a wooden bed, no mattress for comfort, no body, no need. A building with no roof, no doors, just dark. Thoughts to escape my surroundings, to get out of that building. In the darkness, the shape of the trees, awareness of flowers, a garden, no boundaries. No escape, just darkness I likened that place to a prison and a courtyard.

It is said there is no time in our world. Let me tell you the darkness was a lifetime; just my thoughts for company. Surely, gradually, the darkness fades until all is light. A garden of splendour was wasted on me, flowers ripped out of the ground in anger only to return. As time goes by, I became aware of the beauty of the flowers, a fragrance not known before, birds would sing. There is talk on earth that a robin on earth is a loved one drawing close. I would sit in my garden of beauty, a robin would perch on my shoulder. As time progressed, as stepping out of my garden there was a bridge, I felt an emotion never felt before – fear. I would not step on that bridge. In time, a step closer and closer to stand on that bridge, and the fear evaporated. On crossing that bridge there were my family – my wife, my son, my daughter.

I looked back, there was no bridge, no garden, no home; there was no going back. There was just embracement from my family this was alien to me. Tears of joy, tears of love; tears were virgin to me. My visit is short, never to return. The point of my visit, love will conquer to emerge from the dark. Not to confuse darkness of evil where evil was ever present, that fight will continue. The dark of our world and the darkness of evil is a separate world entirely. My parole will continue for light years.

On a personal level for myself, my learning has been great remorse oozes from my soul. Only when my parole is over I will meet my father, mother and sister.

I will embrace them with love.

From Walker, goodbye.

04-10-2019   TRIAN

Welcome, friends, for I am Trian.

My position in life, a General in the Roman Empire. The purpose for my visit? You may compare the difference of Walker and myself. For, like Walker, I took human life, but I followed orders. Life was not taken in battle, for I was a great tactician – when to deploy arrowheads, the spikes of fear, to outmanoeuvre, to outflank, charge and retreat. Yes, I would take the coward's way out and order lower ranks to take life. Forget what your history books say. Arrowheads take out the animal and bring down the man, a single horse can kill four or five men in one go.

Disease took my life, my lungs, to die a slow, painful death. In those dark days I would think it was my torture for taking life. My mother was to outlive me by many years. So proud of her son, for General gave her status and servants in her home. The Roman civilisation – a cruel empire – on my death status removed from my mother, her later years spent in poverty. Like Walker, I was in a dark, plain building, so foreign to me, no splendour, no riches, the likeness a garden with no boundaries, with no escape.

The difference, there was day and night. The day was short, the night was long, but over time the light grew more and more. I was so at peace in that garden. The splendour of the flowers, the birds would perch on my shoulders and on my open palms, the trees would welcome me with each dawn. Full of peace and time for remorse it was never easy taking life, orders had to be obeyed.

In a short time, there were bridges – not one, but three. I was in no rush to cross over a bridge, and there was no fear. Each bridge was identical, I would sit on my plain wooden bench and gaze at each one. Which one to cross? The right, the centre, or the left? One dawn, the change came. To sit and gaze at each bridge, one had turned to stone, one was wood, and the other bewildered me. It was there but it was not there; I could see straight through, for it was transparent.

Still there was no rush but I was so drawn to the transparent bridge. To touch, there was no solidness, just energy. An energy so fierce, to be near the bridge I became alive. I could see what lay ahead but the time had come to step onto that bridge, only for it to disappear. There was no turning back, no home, no garden, no flowers, no trees, no birds. There was just a vast hall with white ivory columns., I was back, I did not want to be there!

I did not want to see the lives I had taken, the ivory floor stained in blood. Do not show me this and it was wrong to obey orders. I was on my knees, my heart ached, so full of grief. The sun is breaking through the ivory floor and columns are melting before me. The blood drains away, the sun is fierce, the green fields grow, the trees return, love fills my heart. 'Is that you, Lord? Forgive me. Mother, lead me, mother take me home.'

I recognise this garden; I recognise the home. So happy to share my life with my mother. She has a herb garden which she tends each day. My bench is there and my favourite flowers. They are red with the colour of blood, with a golden cross in the centre. The cross of each life I have taken, the cross of forgiveness. I have chosen to stay in the garden and pray each day in front of each flower. Although I am forgiven, I still pray and ask for forgiveness. To take life is the biggest crime. Yes, I can wander to other realms. It is my choice to stay, it is my choice to stay with my mother in our paradise and kneel to pray. I know I was touched by our Lord, who brought my mother to me. Understand one thing: I came to our world full of remorse. There was the difference for Walker, for Walker had to learn how to love, how to feel, love and learn remorse.

This is unique to me, to feel the love of another human, for I have touched the love of Master Peter. The journey is different for every soul upon their return. My choice to stay and never to return. I will leave you with the knowledge, a knowledge you will understand, the love inside each one of you. The human mind cannot take the intensity of the love that you hold. I am happy to return, knowing that beauty lies ahead.

It was an honour to be with you all, we shall not meet again. Know that I am happy to have the love of my mother, my blessing goes with you.

Know that God travels with you, God travels with you for eternity.

My blessing for you, goodbye.

28-10-2019   JANE

Hello, my dears, my name is Jane.

Plain Jane, as I was always called at school but let me tell you, there was nothing plain about my two beautiful daughters, Annabel and Louise. I grew up in a beautiful part of our world – New Zealand. I married a farmer, a wonderful man – Alan, a sheep farmer, we met at a barn dance. My work was at a law firm as an administrator, Alan worked the farm. In a short time, I became pregnant, much to the delight of Alan. 'If it is a boy,' he says, 'I shall name him Louis; if a girl, Annabel.'

So, Annabel was born, 7lbs 2oz, and life continued until I was pregnant again. Alan again wanted a boy, so Louis became Louise. Throughout their childhood, Annabel had no interest in the animals – only Shep, one of our two dogs (the other Floss). Shep was so protective towards the girls when they were young.

Annabel was all for education. A first class honours degree, she became a top solicitor working for the same law firm as I. Louise worked the farm with her dad, life was simple, life was good… until tragedy struck. Alan had a heart attack out in the field, Lou blamed herself, for she tried to resuscitate him but he was pronounced dead at the hospital.

But life moves on and Lou required help on the farm. She was left to interview candidates; they were all male, except one. Lou said to me, 'Mom, I saw the hunger in her eyes, the passion in her eyes when I was her age.' So Lou and Joan became a team, and the farm ran like clockwork, like a well-oiled machine.

Life moves on, Annabel married. It was a happy and sad occasion, for her dad not to be able to walk her down the aisle, so I thought, but he was there. Very soon Annabel became pregnant – surprise, surprise, she had a boy whose name was Alan.

Many years later, I retired, I spent most of my days in the kitchen. I loved that kitchen – we were on our third Aga! The same wooden bench, same wooden table, all the carvings of age where I would sit and write children's stories, book after book after book.

We had Betty, a short-nosed pig she was my companion, the kitchen was her home. I awoke as normal, aged eighty-seven years and thirteen days, my dressing gown was folded over the chair. I rose and put on my dressing gown, I entered the kitchen and there was Alan. How could this be? He turned, smiled and said, 'You're home.' It was like being stunned, 'How can this be?'

'You are not alive, look at your hands,' he said. I looked down, the moles had gone, the wrinkles and the veins. I did no more but turned around and went back into the bedroom and picked up my mirror. The long, grey hair had gone; it was brown and healthy. The reflection looking back at me was vibrant and young. 'How can this be?'

I turned to Alan and he said, 'You are home.' I could see Annabel sitting on the floor playing with our grandson.

Alan said, 'You can return anytime you wish.' Then he took me to the fields where Lou and Joan worked. 'You can return anytime you wish.'

'Where am I, Alan?' Again, he said, 'You are home, come with me', he took my hand, 'We are going to the library.' It was a very small library, but the inside was vast, with many, many floors as far as I could see. He pointed to the third floor. 'Look,' he says, 'there is your life, paperback books. These are for you only, no other can read these books.' My life from one year to eighty-seven years.

Alan said, 'You can have a choice to sit in the kitchen and write children's stories that only you will read, or you can sit in this vast library under your section and write your stories that children here can read.' My heart was filled with joy and a love I can't explain. How can a love be so intense when I was so happy with my life before? Alan led me to another part of the library. He dare not read these books, for they were my dad's books and further on, my mom's. 'Where are they, Alan?' I asked. 'Ask for them, and they will be here.'

So strange for my mom and dad to be with me. There were tears, but no tears. My thoughts were, this is going to take some getting used to! I was the only one of our family to work in the great library. We all come together in the kitchen and sit around the table. The table with all the carvings, memories locked away in wood. So many sections in that library, empty, but each section has a name.

My transformation was simple, I passed in my sleep. I awoke and everything was as it should be, as I thought. Each passing is different, each circumstance is different.

Alan has allowed me to tell you of his experience. He woke in the field with Lou shouting and screaming at him. He put his arms around her. 'Calm down, Lou, what's wrong?' Then he explained it being like a movie in slow motion. He stood there and could see himself lying with her shaking him, he knew then that he was home. He tried many times to comfort Lou in her dreams. Only once did he succeed; only then did she accept it was not her fault.

Yes, Master Peter, he saw what you saw – the vortex of light swirling, the bright light, white and black swirling, swirling, drawing me like a giant magnet until all the white had turned to black, he was home. Shep and Floss were there to greet him, he was their Master.

I will leave you with this, we sit in the kitchen around the table. In the centre of that table is like a movie of all the family we visit. To feel the love, the joy and the heartache, for in that kitchen is our time. For you all have your time. Alan and I hold on to Lou, who found happiness eventually. Betty returned to Lou, the short-nosed pig. Life is twofold in our world; it matters not, they are not aware when we return.

You have choices to move objects, what you would call a 'calling card'. There is a transition period, at your gathering, for you to see your return is so very, very different for each individual. Be aware when a loved one has passed and there is a newborn to the family, the loved one is always there.

To look back on my life in those early days, wanting to be beautiful, my adult life was surrounded by beauty. Yes, it's difficult, but try and look at the beauty that surrounds your lives. For I will place a pumpkin in the middle of your circle for the pumpkin has more beauty than the most beautiful flower you can imagine. It is plain to look at, but what is its purpose? That is far, far more important than the look on the outside.

My dears, I thank our world, the Masters for allowing me to be with you. Farewell, my friends, I am around.

Farewell.

08-11-2019   REGGIE

Hello, Reg here.

Reg to the men, Reggie to the lasses, County Down, Ireland, my home – a stoic country. A miner, as my father before me; a family man – three sons and two daughters – proud of every one of them, even the black sheep of the family. We will talk of her later!

It was a normal working day down the pit. It all happened so quickly. A loud rumble, the dust thick, lungs burning, instincts kick in to curl up in a ball and cover the face. Time stood still as though I had a dream, an illusion, for a man stood there in casual clothing – trousers, shirt, and jumper. A pleasant face, a smile so wide, his words, 'Everything will be OK, you will be fine.' All slow motion, the minutes seemed like hours, the dust settled and there was loud moaning.

Thomas, the young one, his leg was badly damaged. The screams haunted me as we bound those legs together. A belt was used as a tourniquet to tighten that buckle, the screams were louder still. We were not to know it was a minor collapse that trapped Shamus, Thomas and myself. Within hours we could hear the noises, loud machinery, air hole produced, time stood still.

The next thing I knew I was lying in a hospital bed with an oxygen mask. 'Where are Thomas and Shamus?' I asked. 'They're ok,' came the reply, days later Thomas' mom visited. She spoke of his ramblings of a man, not in overalls, saying, 'You'll be fine, you'll be OK.'

Doctors told her it was the anaesthetic from surgery. Months went by before I mentioned it to Tom. 'The man you saw…' His reply was, 'You saw him, too', as Shamus also. It was not spoken of again. On our recovery, we became surface workers, not to enter the pit again. The damage was done; damage to the lungs, outward scars. Thomas carried a slight limp and the sadness stayed with me until my return home.

My daughter left home at the tender age of seventeen, mixed with bad ones, addictions took hold, I never saw her again. On returning to our world, I was allowed to re-join her life from seventeen to the present day. To watch the fight, the battle with drugs and anorexia, until her husband-to-be Michael – her saviour, a rock of a man. He could not help her with the unexplained, for he had no answers.

That is where I begin, my daughter loved the Dorset coast, it was 19th May 1973, she sat on the beach watching her children play in the sea, her son Paul and her daughter Marian. She decided to go for a paddle, taking a few steps across the sand, she stopped suddenly. For written in the sand were the words 'KERRY' a heart, and 'LOVE, DAD'.

She did no more but call her children and pointed to those words in the sand. Then she said, 'Paul, did you write this?' 'On Sister Mary's life, no mom.' She asked Marian the same 'As God is my witness, no.'

She did no more but turn and sit and watch as the tide wash those words away. Those words were gone, I wiped them from her mind.

Her home was in Sunderland, where she worked as a receptionist at a GP surgery, the pride swelled up inside of me. Weeks passed as she sat in her lounge reading a medical journal, for she was dedicated to her work. A small white feather floated down and landed in those open pages. She looked up and for a split second she thought she saw her dad. Only then did the floodgates open, day after day, night after night. Michael didn't know what to do, he was helpless!

He could not explain, just hold her tight. She would kneel at the foot of her bed with the Rosary and pray, 'Father, forgive me for the wrath I have caused my family.'

In our world, the energies are always subtle, the signs are always there. At times they are ignored, at times not noticed. My actions caused pain, only to heal pain as within months she was in contact with her sisters and her mom, whose mind was vacant – dementia had taken hold. On visits to mom, the eyes of the soul would recognise and go back to childhood memories and talk to a child and not an adult.

My purpose is twofold, you can do wrong, return home and correct that wrong. A wrong can always be put right from the physical world or our world. A two-way channel, there are those on your world that have that gift to stand in front of a mirror and gaze into the eyes, the eyes that can look back at you and correct a wrong.

The mine to collapse was the best thing that happened, as that man stayed with me all of my life, unexplained but explained, Shamus buried him. Thomas and myself would sit in the corner of our lounge and discuss over a quiet pint. The saviour Christ in another form. For that man was never to return, but never left our minds. He held that ache like an anchor.

Thomas and I were inseparable; separated by age only. For Thomas became so wise he gave lectures, he travelled the country to many mining towns to talk of that man who was our saviour. There was no ridicule, only silence, as miners and their families would listen.

Thomas was to pass as the clock turned midnight. Before that clock was to strike five past midnight, I was to follow – the same hospital, different rooms. Two families came together in grief. Grief and an outpouring of happiness to know that two brothers joined together for a crisis on earth joined together in death. There is not a day that goes by that our daughter does not talk to us in prayer with rosary beads between her palms. For me, the turnaround of her life was nothing short of a miracle.

A simple thankyou to Michael, for he would kneel and pray alongside. That day, a small feather floated down and landed on the bed where his hands lay in prayer. He looked at Kerry, she looked upwards, and said, 'Thank you, dad.' Prayers answered all round.

Do not forget the power of prayer. Know that your life in the physical world may not turn out as you wish. Know there is a correction in our world. You may think of the man who appeared as an earth angel. He is a messenger, a messenger from our world. That is their purpose, the form will change. All of you who work with our world receive a gesture that is unique to yourselves only.

This, Master Peter, is for you to know. If the physical does not work before your passing, it is not for us to say. You can right that wrong, as I know and you know.

I will leave you with this my passing from a hospital bed to a copper mine, clad in my orange overalls and helmet, standing with the Saviour, the man returned. He offered his hand, I took it, I was home. All around love for them and for me.

No physical tears; no, the tears were there for me. It was a pleasure to be with all of you. See me withdraw as the fading light of a candle.

Farewell.

22-11-2019   CLAIRE

Hello, everyone. I'm Claire.

When Reginald started to withdraw, I came in and registered with Master Peter. That's what we do; we register. My life was so different from Reginald's, his childhood, second-hand clothing was all he ever knew, second-hand shoes passed down. Passed on to other families and received from other families. The food I would have thought of as coarse – mutton, belly draft, pigs trotters, bread and dripping.

When Reginald was of an age to earn money, his first set of shoes were brand new, he felt like a prince. I was made to look at my life on my return home, how privileged it was. But at that time it is normal; what we are born into was normal, I was a 'snob'. My life in Swindon, beautiful countryside in a rambling property, twelve acres of land, outbuildings and stables. From the age of four, on my birthday I had my first pony, Jess – a gentle pony. The love of horses was my life. Both my parents were doctors, only the best was good enough for their only child. Clothes that were tailor-made, nothing off the peg, that would be far too common, and of course, only the best education.

My love of horses took over my life. As a young girl, only small hurdles to jump, as Jess was only tiny. Dressage became my love, Henry my horse, I trained him. He would never, never disobey me, that was our downfall. I became a junior champion with Henry, rosettes and cups, we had to be first – second was never good enough. I was so driven; friends didn't come into it. Henry was my only friend until that day, that day that haunted me for so many years. A routine practice to warm Henry up, the hurdles were not high. Was I complacent?

I recall crashing and falling. I awoke in a hospital bed, put into an induced coma. My leg was crushed – bone, sinew, nerve crushed – and my pelvis fractured in three places. I was a complete mess. The next two years seemed like an eternity. Operation after operation and skin grafts. I was never left alone, for the depression was deep, the despair.

Many years on, I was to learn so much. When there is no hope, just despair, the learning is so great. I was born a fighter never to give in, that was my fortune. Never to ride again, a long absence from education, including private tutoring to catch up. Half of me was there, half of me was not.

I also remember the day that changed my life again for the good. That phone call from a child, a six-year-old, Bethany asking me to teach. 'Beth, my dear, it is impossible, I simply cannot ride.' The reply from a six-year-old was, 'Your body may not work but you can still speak.' My parents encouraged me to meet Beth, and there it all started again. My wheelchair was too big, too clumsy, and too heavy. Custom-built to be made, a light alloy, wheels that would snap on and off, designed for hard and soft ground. And there it began, teaching from a wheelchair. News got out, and before long a teenage girl, head of a teaching school.

I was to learn so many lessons. Not to drive those children as I drove myself. In competitions to come second or third deserved praise. Even not to be staged at all, to enter was good enough. A lesson in life, just try your best.

The dream fades, the dream I had as a young child, to go to the Olympics and to be the best. To realise to be the best is so false… to be the best for whom? I asked permission from Reginald to observe his life, I have chosen to return to earth. You may think I'm mad, I have chosen a life of hardship.

To have a life, to be a spoilt brat and know no different. I don't blame my parents; they only wanted the best for their child. It's only on going home that we have that choice. To visit our life and others, only with their permission. I want to get my hands dirty, I want to appreciate the money in my pocket, appreciate the clothes on my back, have friends of my own age, lifetime friends. Only then, through teaching, will I learn friendship. For I could not see past four legs. The love for Henry was not wrong, for love for an animal can be more powerful than love for a human. I was like a horse with blinkers. That was wrong. That fateful day with Henry was the best day of my life, that was the greatest fact to understand.

My message to you all: when there is despair, know there is a future. There are others that wish to speak. I take this opportunity to thank Master Peter for this opportunity to speak. It is such a privilege for all of us to communicate.

My blessings on you all.

22-11-2019   MARK & ADELE

Hello, I'm Mark, I come with Adele. I speak for Adele and myself, for Master Peter has seen us both. He viewed us both as looking at all of you. We need his help, rescue work; we are trapped.

My Adele was deaf, also dumb. She was persecuted, people don't understand. To live in terror, to call her a 'freak'. I refuse to move on and leave her behind. Coventry, Bishop Street, Coventry graveyard – help us, Adele is stuck! Adele refuses to move on, those have tried. We have been given permission from those higher up than ourselves. You speak of Michael as one of the Masters. We called on Michael, he has given us permission to speak on this day, as saviour and friend.

For Adele deaf and dumb and I starved of oxygen. I was called a freak and ridiculed. Was I wrong to take Adele's life then my own? Adele pleaded with me, a pillow to smother her face. They found us, Adele lying peaceful, myself hanging. Only Helen to attend her funeral in an unmarked grave. There are others.

Two graveyards, they would not put us together in death. To roam those graveyards, tired, so weary, so weary. Oh, to return home for Adele to receive love. This effort has been immense for me.

God bless and thank you.

13-12-2019 ADAM

Hello, I'm Adam.

It's my turn to tell my story. On the return home we review our life. As far as I was concerned, I was an all-round good guy. A good husband, son, and father. But do we view us as others see us?

My childhood spent mostly with my grandfather, I think my dad was a little jealous at the time. My grandfather was an expert with motorbikes. He could take the gearbox apart and put it back together, almost with his eyes closed, I loved my grandad. The three of us have one thing in common – football. Grandad, dad and I over the local park. My grandad, dad, and me versus the other lads – great fun! I was to progress to become a professional football player, standards very high. I'm still proud of that fact. I played for Accrington Stanley and a short spell at Shrewsbury Town.

My dad drummed into me 'A short career, son.' So I started taking an apprenticeship, a tool-maker, precision work. Looking back, my precision was my downfall, everything had to be exact. On the football field defensive, barking my orders out, I always took defeat the wrong way. A short career, an ankle injury.

In time I replaced Sunday league football. But onto my passing. A Yamaha 250cc; it was a spring morning, weather dry, clear visibility, or so it would seem. Approaching work, a built-up area, I was travelling

30 miles per hour – I was always the sensible driver – a car came out of a side road, straight into me. It was instant. My explanation of passing, I wasn't sure where I was.

Was I in a cloud? A bubble? Fluffy white light everywhere, it was almost like being wrapped in cotton wool. He seemed to walk through the cotton wool, my grandad. He took me by the hand and said, 'Come on, Ad.' That's what he called me. Would you believe it, I was walking across a football field? We go into the changing rooms, and there the transformation was complete. I met my friend who also passed in a motorbike accident.

There, grandad led me to this doorway. I was so nervous. 'Grandad,' I said, 'what's on the other side of that doorway?' 'Your life, go on, Ad.' The other side of the doorway was a plain room, the white wall, and one chair. I sat there looking at the white wall, then my life unravelled before me. All those forty-two years. I sat there thinking 'This isn't too bad', then I started to watch and realised being perfect was driving my family round the bend.

Trouble started with an extension on the home. I'd stand over the builders, watching them. 'That's not done properly. I want it done this way.' Before long the builder left for another builder to come along, and again the process started. 'I want that corrected.' Our work wasn't halfway through and that builder left. Poor Judy was distraught. 'Not to worry, love, I'll finish it, I'm capable.' But the work only started after my Sunday football, so it dragged on and on.

When it was completed, I was so proud. 'Judy, it's wonderful, you've got the kitchen you've always wanted.' Things went from bad to worse. The worktops were my pride and joy. 'Don't leave wet plates on there, always use a cutting board, don't do this, don't do that.' The house had to be pristine. Little did I realise the damage I was causing. I took over the vacuuming, the washing, and the polishing. I can hear you all thinking that would be good. It drove Judy round the bend, but I couldn't see it. What was I doing wrong?

I was always a cheerful chap, well liked. My insane compulsions drove a wedge between me and my family. It's a small thing, but a big thing. Life is too busy to take stock and look at yourself. You would not believe what I do now.

With these qualities of being exact, being perfect at everything, you would call them lowlife; the lowlife of the earth. I work with those who have no respect for life. I am seen with my qualities to right many wrongs. One quality – my cheerfulness – always sees me through. I always see good in everyone and everything. The emphasis for you all is to see good and break through the barriers that they put up. I'm proud to say I'm doing a good job.

Grandad has brought in an understanding for Judy to see what I do. That has helped Judy to see glimpses of herself, to make sense of her own frustrations. Judy talks to me every day, my ashes kept in the garden. Through grandad, I have instructed him to tell her to move on. She insists there will be no-one else. This may be strange to say to you all: Grandad keeps an eye on my family. I stay with those who are more important. Grandad is my go-between, my messenger. There is no sadness in my tale. A relatively short journey on earth, but a good one.

A pattern unfolds, as Mark has opened the floodgates, a channel open direct to 'SUNRISE'. There will always be those on earth wishing to hear from loved ones. A loved one has a choice to return to visit only, return for another life, or not to return at all – as my choice. Those who don't return, they have a messenger. It is a difficult thing to do to step outside of yourself and analyse yourself. We are far, far from perfect. Judy said to me at that time, 'You are not perfect.' I would have disagreed, as I was the perfect husband, father, and friend.

Until I viewed my life upon returning home, even those who were known as 'lowlife' in time will have a purpose in our world to be proud of.

That conveyor belt never ends, now the door that Mark has opened. Keep happy thoughts, my friend, keep happy thoughts, come together as families. As we come together at this special time, remember it's not what you receive, it's what you give. Give with love. Adam.

Farewell.

13-12-2019   CAROL

PLEASE, PLEASE, help me find my BABY! My name is Carol, my baby taken away from me. My baby's name is Sarah. Pain, screaming pain, childbirth, panic, panic, haemorrhaging. They took my baby away. Searching, searching.

Sarah evil, Sarah taken away to die, left to die, Sarah was placed inside another. The pain was getting weaker and weaker, dark descended, I was floating. I could see Sarah, no blanket, I was screaming and shouting. The doctors were working on me. Leave me, leave me, help my baby!

I was floating, higher and higher, until I sat in a room with a white silk gown around me. I was not to know at that time the gown was to heal and comfort me, my mind was blank. If you think of an induced coma on earth, that would be the best to describe. I was blank, it seemed like an eternity. When the mind could filter images, a strange white figure appeared. There was no pain, no hurt, just love, serene.

I became aware I was in the healing sanctuary. The time came to look at my life up to the point of giving birth, only to find my child is not home. I am so grateful to Mark, for the channel remains open to allow me to find my baby, to be complete. For I have not been able to move on in our world. You should know that not all in our world can move on, if there is an attachment to our earth. We hear so many stories of love and happiness; they are many.

As I said, there are those who are attached to earth, if I can describe it as an attachment that will not go away. There was and still is a practice on earth where a child is sewn into another body, two souls entangled together. There are double souls on earth that attract, for one restricts the release of the other. I ask of you this day for the releasement of Sarah and Thomas – the channel leads to the centre of your gathering. I am calm, for I know very soon Sarah will be with me and Thomas, too. I ask of you upon closing the circle to close completely, then unite hands and ask the power inside your heart to separate the souls of Sarah and Thomas and unite them, it is that simple. A request you will do again and again on a grand scale.

At your next gathering you will invite many, many souls. Do not underestimate the power that lies within the heart, words are not enough. Mark has fought and fought for the channel he has created.

My energy fails, I go home in the knowledge my search is over, already the ache diminishes. Looking forward to your next gathering, many will be here. Many, many, many will follow this channel. Goodbye, my friends, I will thank you all personally when you have gathered in our world.

Goodbye.

03-01-2020   GODDESS AQUA, MICHAEL

Greetings, Goddess Aqua here.

I require no permission to be here, I have free rein to travel where I wish, for I answer to the source only. This day is special for earth. For earth only, the alignment is not exact. I will return in a few moments to allow another to speak.

Hello, I'm so excited to be here, to communicate with you. I left mom and dad just after my 10th birthday – ten years and two days. They so wanted me to meet my tenth year. Around the bed, balloons, birthday boy, and a picture of Ted. I was a bit too old to have a teddy; he now sleeps in bed with mom and dad. That birthday, so much laughter and so many tears.

We had permission for the family to be there. The nurses were wonderful. I think I fell in love with one of them, Pauline was special, so caring, so lovely. I fell asleep, it was so peaceful and waiting for me was my great-gran, Elsie. I didn't know her yet I did, for I recognised her straight away.

Mom always kissed me on the head before I went to bed and she has kept that ritual with Ted. I will get through to her one day. I would like her to take Ted to a charity shop so Ted can have the love of another child and help Mom to stop grieving. Fifteen years have passed; it's time to let Ted go. My earth life was short but happy.

My message to you all: fulfilment in our world is special. I have been allowed to speak as a learning process. I will return to a similar gathering, time in your years about fifty. I will tell those who sit there of all my experiences, all the wonders of this world. I am still a child. The point of my return is to allow me an avenue to make mom aware. I will gain the energy that is required. The Goddess Aqua has notified me to say goodbye.

Greetings, I am Goddess Aqua.

I thank you all for the experience. Today was the beginning of huge, great importance, something immense, the opening of a channel staying as long as the last of this group exists. On the visit to Coventry, sprinkle holy water. The dam has now broken and opened for many souls to be released.

Goddess Aqua has returned and spoken, the alignment has been made. Now work can take place, meaning the great channel was opened which allowed so many souls to pass through. There will be many more channels opened around the world; circles will be opened in all countries and this world.

Farewell.

07-01-2020   GODDESS AQUA

Greetings, Goddess Aqua here,

I tell you of the importance of your last meeting, no less important than those who spend their lives with you. The reason Michael came through as a ten-year-old, for his mother would not recognize those energies if he came through as an adult. The experience to communicate as a ten-year-old holds him in good stead to communicate directly with his mother and father, to end that grief and repair the relationship between them. Small, in the matter of the universe, but all dots put together are very significant. Who is to say that one is not as important as the masses?

Another thought for you all: each channel alters to a degree; information differs from each channel. This channel is here to serve, as all channels are. There is the ego, which must be in place to a certain degree. The ego develops differently in each channel; therein lies the mystery, the mysteries of your universe.

Master Peter has said the channel is open and souls will gather at each gathering. My purpose is to oversee the safe passing, even stubborn ones cannot resist if I am present. They assemble and wait – both gates open at each gathering and close at each gathering. This will be so.

God bless you all. God's blessings on this work.

Farewell.

07-02-2020   GODDESS AQUA

Goddess Aqua, no need for introduction, you know who I am.

I speak about the ants, they lived in a world, Exhalia, in perfect serenity. They live for each other, with no official leader. They each have their own job and purpose. This planet and the way they live will last for ever.

This man had a list of instructions, which later he said he had completed and even more. He mentioned a city beneath the sea, in the past. In life, he had skin as thick as a rhino and as cold-hearted. On his return to the spirit world, he found himself in a wooden hut with rotting wood and a colony of ants. He watched them daily and how they worked as a collective, collecting rotten wood and bringing it back to their nest.

Eventually, the day came when one single ant climbed up his foot onto his shin. He then climbed the mountain, up to the palm of his hand. He then realised that he had not had the sensation to crush the ant between his finger and thumb, as he normally would have done. That is when the tears he cried the first time ever, even as a child. The tears landed on the palm of his hand. He then noticed the ant drank from the tears. From then on, everything changed: the hut disappeared, the grass was green, the birds were singing, and there was an abundance of flowers. He was then embraced by two hands – they were his mother and father.

He then gave each of us the gift of energy into the palms of one of our hands, for healing. We were instructed to use this energy on the brow of those we heal. We can use this energy on ourselves, to activate our third eye gifts – telepathy. We can begin to send telepathic thoughts to members of this circle. As he said farewell, he believed he could consider us his circle of friends. He finally gave his Christian name as Rupert. His heart had opened and we thanked him. The people of Exhalia, the mind so varied, think on a global scale. No matter how far they travel, a stranger is treated as family. There is respect, a planet with great respect.

Farewell.

06-03-2020 GODDESS AQUA

Greetings, friends and followers, this is Goddess Aqua.

The mention of the flame. It grows larger and larger, and is seen beyond the beyond. The flame penetrates the darkness.

First, I will answer a question. What is the Seeth? A Seeth resembles an ant on earth, but larger. It's earth planet is Exhalia, and those that live on Exhalia respect the Seeth, and they live their lives as the Seeths. It would be a great injustice to kill; that thought would never enter their minds. Remember Rupert in that wooden shack, he didn't crush that Seeth between his finger and thumb.

On Planet Earth an ant would be seen as an irritant, a nuisance. If they were to become extinct, what effect would that have? Serenity oozes out of every single pore of the Seeth.

Another question: the Arkwright? Where there is correction, there is an Arkwright. The depth of that correction, it varies for each of those who return. Only when the correction is put right will they move on.

Many have paid tribute and given thanks in the culture of their belief. Now I move on to allow another to speak. On our next meeting, reach out to the skies.

Farewell.

06-03-2020   GILL'S SISTER

Everyone, I'm so excited to be with you, born in Surrey, my parents said I was a problem child. I had speech therapy. I always played up, not like my sister Gill. She was a goody-goody. She played with dolls and teddy bears, she took them to bed. What did I take to bed? A football! I was a tomboy, I didn't play with girls, I played with boys. I loved my footie, playing local neighbourhood teams. At first, they would say, 'We're not having a girl in our team', until they could see how good I was. I could play any position – goal, defence, midfield or forward. It gave me as much pleasure stopping goals or scoring goals.

My parents said I was a handful, so I did them a favour, I left home at sixteen, sweet sixteen! There was nothing sweet about me! I left, Gill was happy, my parents devastated, underage and gone. I love freedom, let the wind blow in your hair.

There was a group of us squatters – that's what we became. Moving on, one house to another, squatters! Only now I know how wrong I was. In those days I looked down on the rich. Empty homes, a couple that were called mansions, they were wrecked. Did we care? No, we didn't! Broken furniture and graffiti on the walls. I was a wild child, a wild teenager, and a troubled adult. Drugs came into play. I never saw my parents again; I never went back. There was a period in my life where drugs had damaged my body – anorexia. Yet it was the best time of my life. You may think, how was that possible? Well, I learnt so much in that time.

In despair, in the darkness, only to come out the other end of the tunnel. To live a life each day is precious. No-one was here to help; my own willpower pulled me through. With the aid of doctors, induced coma, and willpower. I made a promise to myself to look after the remains of my body. I say that I had arms and legs, but damaged inside. I was always one for free love. There are names you call today; I didn't care. In those days, addicted to drugs and sex, a wild child – one thing missing, happiness.

A man found me, I did not find him. Through the determination of getting myself right, finding work, menial work, I had a brain, but no qualifications. I became a waitress. There was this gent sitting reading his newspaper, an ordinary looking man. When ordering his food, his voice penetrated right through me. I was mesmerised by his voice, but he was plain looking. I got to know him, and out of the blue he asked me out for a meal. How my life changed we were to marry – a simple registry office, the ring a cheap band that my daughter wears to this day. We couldn't have children so we adopted a daughter Elizabeth – Beth – my life was complete. Beth was my child, she was barely two months old, we lived in a small cottage, a modest home, a modest garden.

Pansy is my favourite flower. Why Pansies? They smile back at you; they have a happy face. My life, free love, the darkness that my mind could not control, was over. Another chapter found with Tony and Beth. But how we learn from the wrong in our life. Do I regret not seeing my parents? Yes and no, for what torment would

I have put them through, to see what I had become? But then, to see what I became.

This is such a privilege for me to talk to you all. I was never very big – petite is the word, a small frame. It was always said that I was pretty but I could not see that. Contentment to be in my garden, to be surrounded by pansies, in the knowledge that Beth grew up to be a fine adult. She now works as a veterinary nurse. Towards the end of life, we decided to move around in a small caravan. Surrey was an area I avoided, never go back to. Never, never go back over old memories.

There are two sides to every leaf, two sides to every leaf that grows on a tree. Gill was one side, I was the other. Would I change a thing? No! Freedom is what we all wish for. How often do people live their lives as they want to? Conditioning comes in so many ways. I was a rebel.

It is such a pleasure to be with you all. When you are in that moment of despair, think of what you learn, for you will take that with you on your return.

The energies turn anticlockwise, that is my sign to leave. It is my wish to return again. I ask of you just one more thing – to join hands before I go, so that I can feel the warmth and energy of you all.

Bye, bye, my lovely friends.

24-04-2020 GODDESS AQUA, JAMES

Welcome, it is I, Goddess Aqua.

The channel will remain open this day for the animal kingdom. Do not limit your minds, for the animal kingdom includes insects great and small. They in turn pay their respects on their ongoing journey.

As we continue, we do not interrupt that channel. Only briefly will we talk of this mini crisis at this present time. For there have been many learning curves for your earth, and this is just another. Where there is grief and sadness, there is joy and celebration in our world. One will explain the joy and celebration as I stand back and allow that one to speak with you.

James here, thankyou for giving me your time. Affectionately known as Jim, a man of few words, a mind scarred, mental scars deep inside the mind. Before the Second World War, my profession was a civil servant. The war days were never mentioned. On my return home, for many years I carried the thought that I was one of the lucky ones. My unit was the parachute regiment, North of Poland our destination. To push the enemy forward into a trap, our troops lay in wait. It was threefold for our regiment – the casualties, and those that made it back to 'Blighty', and those that spent those years as prisoners.

I was a prisoner, my wife Samantha was informed 'missing in action', so there was limbo. To survive in a prison camp was a living torture and that is all I will say. Only upon my return did I realise I was not one of the lucky ones. How wrong I was. For each year that passed, I would salute my comrades that had fallen and shed a tear.

I awoke, upon my return to the spirit world, in a plain room and there standing in front of me as I lay in that bed, weary, standing to attention, saluting me, were those that were taken. Where am I? How can this be? They were so young. My next visitor was Samantha, she had passed some 31 years before me – cancer took her, as it took me.

I have no wish to return to my old profession. I was not the same, never would be. I had savings, and I opened a small shop – an ironmongers. My son had no wish to join the business. Through life I felt so guilty to watch my children and their children. My grandson Charlie, in the school holidays he would come and work in the shop. He was a quick learner and very good with the customers. A natural process for him to take over the business.

In those early days trying to build a life, the demons inside, when the guilt was so strong, only Samantha was the bridge between life and death. To allow you to understand, to feel guilt is wrong, there is a life far greater than this. A life where there is beauty at every turn, beauty to behold that you can grasp. The mental scars took their time to heal, only then did beauty become apparent.

For my life not seen by my loved ones was false on the inside, how wrong I was. I will leave you in the knowledge that there is a beauty that lies ahead for all. Yes, I will return to earth to live another life. That is a little way off, for all intricacies have to be worked on.

We don't return without knowledge that lies before us. There is a blueprint to work to, and there is an unforeseen destiny. Without that destiny there would be no learning. We all return with knowledge to move on. The roots of knowledge that spread out into our world like tentacles, that work on the airways. I will leave you with a four-leaf clover, and within each leaf there is knowledge.

On the doorway of my shop a horseshoe that will also hang on the doorway of your dwelling. Be assured my friends, beauty and love lie ahead for all. We do not discriminate, but correction will also bring love. Different qualities that we all have, we all have qualities for the right quarter. I salute you for the work you do and the understanding that I have.

Farewell.

Goddess Aqua, my return back to you is to close the channel, as you know time is of no importance. Be told, multi-millions have passed this day, for they pass what you would call the time of life. An understanding that you should have in our world when you return. It has been said, a silly thing: does it not get overcrowded? As those return, others exit our world. It has no boundaries or limits, an expanse timeless and limitless.

There are those that sit in this gathering that confuse my name. I am not the Goddess of water but of soul releasement. We shall talk on the grades on our next visit. Remember the flame never dies.

Farewell.

08-05-2020 GODDESS AQUA, KARL SCHNEIDER, STACEY GOLDBERG

It is I, Goddess Aqua.

One will talk who has passed through this channel. But first, let us talk of the energies, for there are many on your earth. Thermal energies, radial, electric, gas, gravity, sound, movement, and so on. Every single object of solid mass is energy; energy is everywhere. You have the capabilities to send energy soul to soul, for emotions are energy. To send out your energy to another is a form of healing – the human body recycling, the energy is cocooned in an energy of pale yellow. The density depends on the frequency of that energy. We have spoken before that love will never die and love is pure energy.

You see, love is a gesture. Love in the eyes, the window of the soul; love can heal, love can mend a broken heart, yet love can destroy in the wrong quarters. It is said that Jesus was the greatest healer of all. Branch off from Jesus, branch off again and again and again, for all that walk this branch from Jesus and the healing qualities. For love is the greatest energy. Never dismiss love that is sent; distance is irrelevant. On this day where respect is world-wide, there is one I will stand back and allow him to introduce himself.

KARL SCHNEIDER

Greetings, our thanks go out worldwide. Let me introduce myself, I am Karl Schneider. We met our fate in the early years of World War Two, off the coast of Singapore. The crew member of a U-boat, our mission to sink cargo and cargo ships. We would have a time slot for maintenance work on the surface, maintenance being carried out, and then a random attack from the skies. Report minimal damage, within 48 hours we lay on the seabed of the Indian Ocean, mechanical failure.

Captain Reiker was a hero to give his life for his crew. To give them time to repair. The repair was fruitless, as we lay trapped on that seabed running out of air. There were those that cried, those that prayed, and those that wrote to their loved ones. They knew those letters would not be read. But, let me tell you, on their return home to their loved ones, one by one those letters were read and are still read to this day, as the few still return.

This channel is a releasement for the crew members, although we choose to live on Betsy our submarine – our home, our lives, our deaths. We honour you all. We salute all those that fell and those that lived on to return. For on that return it is always the same to salute them in the custom of their country. There are those of us who still return to the bottom of that ocean, back and forth, for Betsy was our love – even to this day, every nut and bolt, hinge, every plate of steel.

Our thanks for you all who sit this day to do your duty like soldiers at war. We are at peace, farewell.

Farewell.

STACEY GOLDBERG

Hello, Ann and Pete, my name is Stacey Goldberg.

I will briefly talk of Rose, my sister. I was a year older than Rose. I was a rebel, but not to quite the same degree. The only thing I had in common with Rose was that I rebelled against my parents, and once I left home I was never to see my parents again.

My story, I grew up in the outskirts of Suffolk – Woodbridge, an affluent part. My mother a lawyer, my father an accountant, they would commute each day to the east of London. I had a nanny who I would call mother, a bond so strong. When I was of age, I was sent to boarding school. My parents purchased a flat to work and live in London. I always thought of myself as an irritant to my parents, for there was no close bond – boarding school, then university. I left without the knowledge of my parents. I found work in a care home. To be with the elderly fitted me like a glove. Life for me was like a rolling stone, content to amble along on one level.

I had a brief relationship with Alan but I never really had any interest in men. I was happy with my own company, to sit and listen to the tales of the elderly. Some would think a lonely life, but not I. I purchased my own little flat, which was my own sanctuary and heaven. I would get lost in books and write poetry; I loved words. I would dwindle those evenings away listening to classical music – Mozart, Beethoven, and many others. I had little to do with neighbours. Some would consider me boring. I had no interest in people my own age, just to care for the elderly and their needs.

There were no surprises. My time on earth, no major events in my life. I was happy, an only child. I was to hear my parents never even bothered to look for me; work was their only interest. How fitting my later stages of life – a stroke limited the body to spend those days in that care home where I worked all those years.

How fortunate that little Suzy was a mirror image of me. She would sit and recite my poetry and wipe away those tears as they rolled down my cheeks. It was not sad when my time came, for at my funeral there was just one. No family, no friends... but Suzy. She was more than a friend – that love that burns so brightly inside, the love that Goddess Aqua spoke of.

For my destiny was to understand love, to give freely and receive love. Suzy is now frail, her legs are weak, she sits in that wheelchair and sleeps most of the day. Suzy has passed on that love to her daughter. I wait for her return.

I will be there, because she will follow on that channel of love. There are those on earth that fear to show love because they feel so vulnerable. I cannot express to you the love in our world. There are those upon their return that take longer for the love to penetrate. Make no mistake, the soul in time will be pure love – only when the correction is complete. My correction was swift.

Do not dismiss, yes, Peter, do not doubt your mind. The one that came in, do not doubt your mind. For yes, you asked the question, and a name, famous on your earth, Adam Faith he did speak to you, Master Peter.

I will also show myself to you. I was blonde, with hair parted down the middle, straight, almost touching my shoulders. I wore glasses, I was ordinary and plain looking. People would pass me by and not notice me, but that was all I ever wanted. To be completely by yourself, to love yourself, as I do, so easy to give out love. There are many who will visit on your return, those that have spoken will introduce and I will stand in line.

Peter and Ann, I forward my love to you both. Thank you for allowing me this time.

Farewell.

22-05-2020   GODDESS AQUA, JACOB

Welcome, it is I, Goddess Aqua.

The channel is now open. We will talk on your next gathering on advancements in health and technology. I will waste no more energy and allow another to speak with you.

JACOB

Greetings, first, I will introduce myself for respect. I am Jacob; my birthplace was Philadelphia. In 1663 my life was to change, and Louisiana became my home. Stock, we were called, I was fortunate for many, many years. Massa Hutchinson would travel to the sea, to Alabama and Mississippi, for 'stock'.

I was born into slavery on a cotton farm. The hours were long, but Massa Hutchinson was a fair man. There were degrees on status. There were those with skills to work with iron, lumber, and those skilful with livestock. The womenfolk were skilled in cooking, sewing, and working in the nurseries. They fared better than those women who worked in the fields. We were allowed to marry and have a ceremony, and when the old passed on we had our own graveyard to bury them in.

Marbella was to be my bride. Our lovely daughter, Iris, was torn away by Masser Hutchinson's son. The Masser would not stand up to him; he was weak. She was 13 years old when the junior Masser used her for his sexual needs. Two grandchildren – a grandson called Jacob, and a granddaughter. Marbella, barely thirty years old when sexual disease ravaged her body, these facts were hidden. When they became ill, there was no return, they would be shot. A horse had more rights than us. For what was a negro? Wastage!

The purpose of my visit: when the Masser passed on, his son changed so many things. To rip down the fence of our graveyard, the simple wooden crosses torn out of the ground. Food was slop, and we worked until we dropped and then to be replaced. Drive them, drive them. I would kneel each night with Marbella and felt no guilt for what I asked for. I asked for the Masser to die. My prayers were answered, for the day came when he drank and drank, his mood was rage. The beatings were many, but that day came, he fell off his horse. Amongst those broken bones, his neck was broken. I had no guilt that he didn't die instantly, two long days passed and he was buried in the family plot.

From then on, life changed, for such an evil man to have such a caring sister, a Mistress with so much respect. For those with the craft of lumber, they built new homes; shorter hours in the fields; those whose hands were riddled with arthritis were given easy tasks. The hate I felt inside on my return home, the correction to dissolve this hate inside.

I had no wish to meet Masser Sam, the evil man, but I was wrong to hate. Masser Hutchinson was there to shake my hand, it was a shock. The respect and love followed by respect and love is our world.

We have now, in our world, our own little farm. My daughter Iris welcomed me. She said, 'Come, Pa, I'm taking you home.' It is hard on your world to dispel hate from your emotions, but you will understand in time.

A great nephew of my grandson Jacob – Jeremiah – was the first to break out of slavery. In the great library, Jeremiah records slavery at its peak until its ending. I have sat and read that book and recalled the good times along with the bad.

With great respect, I bid you farewell.

19-06-2020   GODDESS AQUA, ABDUL

Welcome, it is I, Goddess Aqua. Beware, the energies are so powerful.

It is thanks to the collective, not the individual. The collective from Mark to be recognised in our world, and Adele to never leave his side. They are to become ambassadors to the freedom of the trapped souls. We ask all of you to sit in your own time, a time that suits you. Ask for a channel to be open, for one energy, the channel is smaller; for the collective, it is greater. Let it be known that billions have passed through this channel. That is a mere drop in the ocean, and many drops make up the ocean. For those of you who sit as an individual, allow that channel to open and thousands will pass. This is a new beginning for the three of us to work together.

For the importance of the releasement of souls is twofold. Firstly, to reunite the soul to its home, and secondly to balance your earth. My work is complete at this gathering, to move on with Mark and Adele, for others to become those channels. Know that this channel remains open until the last of you return to your home.

Now, one other will talk with you who has passed through this channel.

I will bid you farewell, we will meet one more time. Farewell.

ABDUL

My thanks go out to this gathering to end the turmoil, to tread the same path over and over, I am Abdul. My papa shamed the family. He was groomed from a young boy to take over the family business, Abdul Furnishings. He was to mix and tangle with a white girl. This is how his family would speak; shamed and pressured, a choice he had to make.

For me, the wrong choice – my momma, a single parent to live in the backstreets of Glasgow; my father never set eyes on me. My regret was to cause constant heartache for my mother. Life was tough as a child, brutal, for names hurt – Paki, scum – graffiti on windows and doors – half breed.

My mother spat on in the street. To make matters worse, to have dark skin and red hair. My life was short – barely seventeen years of age. It was recorded accidental death by drowning. It was a lesson to learn, not to be able to swim. My mother constantly told me keep away from canals.

Tormented that night, 'accidental death' by drowning. I pushed too hard, the voices I still hear. It is impolite to come through and use bad language. 'Drown, you Paki' and laughter as I struggled. Many years I have walked that towpath, the voices and the torment of that laughter. My mother lost the will to live, she refused to eat until her body shut down. There was only my mother at my funeral. There was not one to attend, for the shame on my mother runs through all families.

The relief of this channel for what the collective will achieve. For the troubled soul can't be measured, can't be put into words. The entrapment of the soul, a living nightmare. You may think the spirits of our world should penetrate and return. It takes the energies of both worlds to achieve this, for the entrapment of the soul, darkness lurks. It is darkness that recorded those voices, the darkness that recorded the laughter.

For do you understand, to stand by and allow another to perish there is negativity in the minds? You see it on your earth, day in day out. But know also that I have flourished on my return home. I no longer want to avenge, I no longer want justice for my mother. We live and work together in a modest terraced house. We have one room in that home – a special room for the return of a trapped soul to enter. Call it what you will – a healing room, a therapy room – we sit with that soul until the time to move on, then another soul returns and we sit with that soul, and so it goes on. It is our sanctuary, that little terraced home in Glasgow, in our world.

Those of you who sit in the quiet from this gathering, I ask of you a request. As the souls pass through each individual channel, send one of them to our sanctuary. That is the main purpose of my visit. Through all of you, we continue to work.

Farewell.

03-07-2020   GODDESS AQUA, RICHARD Re: RACHEL

Welcome, it is I, Goddess Aqua.

These words I do not use lightly, welcome Goddess Ann and Master Peter. This may seem a little premature to address you as Goddess, for you came into this world with a set of tasks which are worthy of those on the higher plains only. Upon your return to our world, after correction, adjustment, and rehabilitation, it will be an honour for me to work with you. Mark and Adele will be long gone. Their apprenticeship long over, they work together as one. I will allow another to talk with you. We will speak in a short while.

RICHARD RE: RACHEL

Hello, I was born with the name Richard. I have been given permission for you to address me as Rachel, born into this world as a twin, with a sister Nicole. It is said that the egg in my mother's womb separated, and genes got confused. I was always sensitive as a child and cried easily, Nicole was the opposite. We were of the days where parents were allowed to punish. I would always cry; Nicole never shed a tear.

Our toys: I would play with Nicole's dolls, she had no time for dollies. She grew into a tomboy, a tomboy to play football with the boys. I always played with the girls. Great confusion for my mother and father. As we grew, my father in particular found it very difficult.

These words will always comfort me. He would say, 'I love you, son.' To that day, where he lay in his bed with pneumonia – my mother one side, Nicole and I the other – as he said, 'I love you all.' Tears ran down my mother's cheeks, and my cheeks also; Nicole's eyes dry as anything. I always held those words close.

Those days when life was very difficult, sports days I loathed. I hated my body, for I had huge hips. I was far taller than boys my age, it was only my height and size that stopped me from being bullied. Nicole was tall and slim; how I envied her. We were both gifted in our own right. Nicole excelled at art, where I excelled at maths. Figures, I adored them; mathematical problems, I was a whizz. In time, Nicole grew into a lady, in time I grew into a lady also.

As children, I would dress up in Nicole's clothes, but they would not fit. In adulthood, men's clothes would not fit, Nicole was my saviour. She designed clothes and had a seamstress friend, all of my clothes made to measure, I stood six foot one-and-a-half, huge hips and broad shoulders; Nicole 5ft 11 and slim. I used to pull her leg, 'It was my doing, your good fortune.' For designing my clothes, a top designer saw Nicole's work. I became a reluctant part-time model, short lived, but suited me fine. Nicole went on to design. I was an accountant to wear a suit, shirt, and tie. To make them bearable, designer undies – ladies, of course. Yes, I had relationships, all cloak and dagger, they all fizzled out.

Unlike Nicole, she was very sociable. She loved the limelight and the pressure of work. I was content in my own company, many years celibate, many years happy with my lot. For after work I would change into a frock and drink herbal tea. I never once travelled; I was content in my home and in my garden. My neighbours did not judge. They saw the beautiful soul trying to escape. For we are born into this world some would call a freak of nature. It is wrong to be attracted to the same gender? As my father would say to me, 'Above all, son, be happy. If you find love, grab it by the throat and never let it go.' The love I found was the love of my family. For Nicole, she never shed a tear but she was not cold or hard. She would visit frequently, she would kiss me on the cheek and say, 'Rachel, my sister, I love you.'

My purpose of this visit: don't judge, look past what lies on the outside. My work in our world, I work with those who were starved of love. To understand the difficulties, you had to have been there, experienced it. I had the love of my family; that is a different love.

Yes, Master Peter, I have worked with your mother. It is not disrespectful of me, Lady Ann, to call you sweetie. That is how I would have addressed you. Friends were few, but the close friends I always referred to as sweetie. Nicole would know when she called, paying one of her visits, if I did not call her sweetie, she would ask what was wrong.

My blessings, and know that all the difficulties, to be trapped in the wrong body, I always try to see the good and send love to all those that didn't understand me. The day will come when judgement will not take place. I am free to roam and roam, and I will.

My thanks to this gathering, for all you do for this world, and respect to all.

Farewell, farewell.

GODDESS AQUA

I ask of you all, all those that have visited this gathering and spoke of their lives and the challenges they faced, the differences in all walks of life, I hope you have gained a little knowledge from each of those.

There is too much concern on this earth: what will be, will be! Man will continue to advance, the earth will become lighter and lighter as the pull of gravity leads its way. There will always be darkness, there will always be light, but the light will always prevail.

All those that have spoken at this gathering are here today and standing to the right. At the front are Mark and Adele. Let it be known what you have achieved with the channel and so many, many souls. On the return of each individual, they will all attend, mark each individual with the sign of the cross.

You have choice, as an individual in our world – not all work, not even those who are qualified in certain fields. If they choose not to work, that is their choice. Freedom of choice is our world. You are set free to soar, to soar the universe of our world.

I bid you farewell, until that return comes.

14-08-2020 ARGOS

Greetings, I am Argos.

My purpose: for decisions to be made by all. But first, it is respectful to talk of my experiences. For I, as a young boy, fought for my freedom to survive. I was taught by my father, a great man in his own right. I became a gladiator, do not get carried away I did not fight at the Colosseum, nor was I famous. We fought in the deserts, the villages of the poor, and the villages of the rich. As time went by, there were three of us Leanna, a female, for what she lacked in men's strength she made up in lightning speed. Then there was Zeon, we were travellers, never resting in one place. One point to make clear to you, we did not fight to kill, we fought to win. For there is no choice if the opponent would not yield, death was swift. My chosen weapons, sword and axe; Leanna, two short-bladed swords, for the weight was evenly balanced; Zeon, a sword and a shield. In his hands, the sword was a fearsome weapon. It was our living to move on, to fight to spill blood, later to be regretted by us all. Our payment came in many forms, to have our tools and weapons maintained, and clothing.

One thing you take for granted in part of your world – water. Other parts people would kill, for what? Every time a life was taken, we would travel and rest. As night descended upon us, we would pray for the soul of that life, for resurrection. The bow was tradition, it was made from yew – a tree you will find in many of your churches and graveyards, for the belief of the yew was death and resurrection.

For those who spoke of taking life, to take life with a long bow there was a belief that resurrection would occur. You may ask the question: why one who returns to this gathering has taken life? We have an understanding to take life, to preserve life, to prolong life. I will talk of a life – no names no explanation – those that are fighting for their life.

I Argos, Leanna, and Zeon are now protectors of life. Those that lie in comas, we are there; for those that fight, we are there, we protect and prolong. For those who show no fight, we are there but we can do no more. The soul looks upon help with the struggle of the human body – a conscious and subconscious signal sent to the soul, which we register. If the fight is not there, we make our exit to allow the chosen one to take them home. Those that fight, the three of us come together and we are formidable. There are times when we cannot fight the decisions of the family. When we are at that point, and the opponent will not yield, the blow is swift to ease the suffering. The decision is not to dwell, but to be decisive when that time comes. Be decisive in other aspects of your life. Our lives were short but now our skills prolong life.

Zeon was first for what you would call retirement, for there were not many gladiators to reach that point. He became a shepherd, he kept goats. I was to trade in animal skins. Leanna was something else – so strong in mind, so strong in her thinking, motherhood was not for her. Her wish was to become the best, but the best becomes a target. Time and age, the hazards of speed, slowing, ebbs away. I was there, a bystander in the dusty desert, to watch her blood stain the sands. That night as darkness fell, a night never to be forgotten, I knelt on those sands, cupped my hands where I scooped up the stained blood in my hands. I held that sand in the palm of my hands as I prayed and the skies appeared to open.

With age I was partly blind but there in front of me – how could this be the Lord? As the tears ran down my cheeks, my eyes became streams of sadness, happiness and relief. She spoke. 'Argos, I am your protector until you return home.' Sleep befell me, and upon awakening it must be a dream, my eyes deceive me. A voice came in loud and clear: 'Tend the goat with the injured leg.' That voice was clear, the accent was clear. My eyes may betray me, but my hearing was sharp.

I know of no goat but I searched and there she was looking at me. I tended the leg and carried her on my back to allow the leg to heal. I spoke to no-one that night of what I saw, or the voice that called out to me to return home. It is for you yourselves to decide on your journey home.

Remember when that time comes, be swift with your decision. It is your life or another. Beauty lies ahead, beauty that cannot be explained. There is a coming together of all worlds, a closeness, the skies will become universal. Overseeing, the Lord Jesus made his presence felt in your time, the blink of an eye. Remember I am a protector, this is not to say you are in danger – you are not, fight, and never give up the fight.

Until the next gathering, this is Argos saying farewell.

25-09-2020   SAMANTHA, EWAN McGREGOR

Hello, I'm Samantha I want to go into the playground. I am dressed in a yellow frock with flowers. My daddy is here, I want to play on the swings and climb the rope ladder. Hi, lassie, or should I say, Lady Ann, Ewan McGregor here. Off you go lassie, go join the children. Bye, Daddy.

EWAN McGREGOR

Don't underestimate lass, the achievement with the great playground – all walks of life, all cultures where children can be children. White Star, who is the stallion, goes down on his knees to allow two to climb on his back, they wait in a queue patiently for their turn.

I am not here to talk on different subjects. This gathering, souls pass at speed, children come in droves, two by two has gone by the board. We have Philip two, James five, Alexander six, Gregory ten, Annabel four, Joe six, Katherine six. Jessica Llewellyn is there to observe, not to control, control is not required; she is a guardian.

The children are so polite. 'Jessica, is it my turn now?' and so on… Jessica has a heart that will never grow old. Children adapted so well. The time will come when other worlds will see the playground. The grass is velvet to the touch, the clouds in the sky are fluffy and comforting. Trees stretch out their limbs to allow the children to scale them. Aye, lass, be proud, for you will visit and see for yourself.

Sally and I, we passed together, drowned at sea. In the panic and confusion, Sally was separated from her mother, Izzy, my love. We come forward this day together, for Sally and I passed together, we have not been apart since. The great playground allows me to move on. I work with all those that passed as we did.

The great window is open, for those on different levels in our world can view the great playground and receive great joy in watching the children play. I honour you for this achievement and allowing me to move on in the knowledge that Samantha has broken free to be amongst her own.

My time with you is brief but the achievement great.

Farewell, lass.

05-02-2021   ANTHONY

I am Anthony, my heartfelt gratitude to communicate with you this day. My absolute respect for Goddess Aqua – she steered me through calm waters, the mist and fog dispersed for good.

I am a simple man, we were simple folk, born and raised in a small town called Welcome, in Louisiana. The eldest, Maureen, myself and Thomas. Thomas and Anthony, we were known as the terrible twins. We regularly played up the elder folk; they took it all in good fun, happy days. Then there was Lotty, in the same classroom, Mrs Briggs was the teacher. Lotty and I were childhood sweethearts.

Maureen helped out at the general store with Ma. Tom and myself worked with Pa at the lumber mill. Tom was born with hearing defects, some thought as backward. The speech was slow but the mind razor sharp. I always looked out for Tom. There was always the three of us. Before the war came along, talk was ripe, the unrest.

Lotty and myself were to wed – a simple ceremony, the church was packed. The call came on that rainy day. I made a pledge to Tom to return; Lotty also pledged to look after Tom.

I was a proud Marine, island-hopping, or so it seemed. The South Pacific 1942, so much blood, friends lost, the fighting was fierce. The curse of the Japanese, mighty soldiers knew no fear. How do you describe what your eyes see all around you? Eardrums pounding, eyes glaring, screams to wake the dead, so vivid and so young. They kept coming, bayonets fixed, charging and screaming coming towards me, we met full on, I fired. The bayonet skewered my side, the mist formed, the fog so dense, the quiet, only for the fog to disperse and the screaming and shouting as we met full on. I fired and the blade penetrated my side. The mist, the fog, the quiet, again and again so real.

My pledge to Tom to keep fighting, to return, fighting, fighting, fighting. Only, on the calling of Goddess Aqua, the fog did not return, my eyes could only see the flame burning so brightly, the pull was strong, and yet the pledge was there but the flame was greater. Beyond that flame awaiting my return, Ma and Pa, Maureen, Lotty, and Tom. How can this be? My arms extend to love them all, as tears flowed; they were real but not real. To one side stood Loko, as he bowed, I saluted him. My pledge kept him fighting also. We returned to the love of our families.

When I was away, Maureen, Tom, and Lotty worked side by side at the lumber mill, long hours to work, many shifts over twenty-four hours, for beech wood was in demand. We all served for one cause, king and country.

This new world so strange, the lightness astounds. The family has grown, for Tom has two sons and two daughters, Zac and Zeth. His humour – Tom and Tony, the two Ts; his daughters, Suzanna (his wife put her foot down), the other Daisy.

My son Archie went on to teach at the local school where Ma and Pa were educated. There is talk in our world of the room you call the therapy room. I place a hand-carved heart in beech wood, with a simple word under that heart – Anthony. Think of it placed under a fish-shaped tambourine. Please place this heart in the centre of your table, in the centre of your circle that you sit around this day.

All those you call photographs in your therapy room – I say portraits – they all send their love. (We have many photographs of friends who have passed away in our therapy room at Sunrise.)

On my return home, I lay there and lined up in rows that the eyes cannot count, all those that had fallen and all those that went on to return.

One thing I ask of you, Lady Ann and Master Peter, in your mind, next to the candle, place a heart of beech, a mark of respect to each soul that passes through. For on their return they will see the flame that burns so bright and the heart also. They will also know that love awaits them. There are so many battles that have gone and are to come. There are those who continue to fight, and the work on your earth will continue to free those souls. Again my heart cannot express the love and the gratitude.

I am aware Goddess Aqua's energy is no longer there. The pull is great.

Farewell, my friends, farewell.

05-03-2021   NICOLA

Hello, Master Peter and Lady Ann, I'm Nicola.

I was asleep in the back of the car, mommy & daddy knew nothing of the car that hit us. They both work now and I play in the golden long grass with Tigger. I remember when he was old and slow; now he is full of energy and chases the ball all day, he loves to search for it. Mommy and daddy are doctors, they now care for those who return. My days are spent with Tigger, catching butterflies to let them go again. I paddle in the crystal waters of the stream and play with the tadpoles as they swim by.

I have a friend Billy, he is sad. He will talk of an explosion that tore his home apart. He is constantly looking for his mommy and daddy. The news, that they are set to return, for they were trapped between the two worlds, Billy will be reunited this day. Not all the children join the playground, for Billy will stay and wait for his mommy and daddy. In their room is a giant Buddha, a golden glow, they will know they are safe. Billy stands and awaits their arrival. It's Billy's time now, I'm off to catch some butterflies. My mommy and daddy will be with Billy. The glow of the golden Buddha reaches where you sit and mirrors the flame.

Nicola says thankyou and goodbye, she's very busy chasing butterflies.

19-03-2021 NO-ONE SPECIAL
BORN IN HUDDERSFIELD

Hello, Master Peter and Lady Ann.

I am no-one special, I was born in Huddersfield. My childhood was hard, I had no education. I had to help with the washing and ironing the clothes of the gentry to deliver by cart with my mother, I also had to clean the house. The turning point in my life, I was to marry Samuel and live with my mother and father. In no time we became nomads in search of work, from town to town, from city to city. Them Gemma arrived, a difficult birth, another mouth to feed.

Until that fateful day both sets of parents scrimped and saved for tickets for the mighty *Titanic* – a wonder for the eyes to see. We were thought of as low-life, sewage, out of sight as the upper deck gentry waved goodbye to their loved ones. Our cabin was tiny, we shared with Serena, Tom, and their little Billy. That night we were unaware of all the raucous above us. We were thrown from our beds and chaos was soon to follow, the noise so loud, of timbers cracking and groaning. How can this be?

I held onto Gemma so tight, as she held onto Rosie, her little doll. Samuel was gone, trying to find help. Water came in from every angle. The cold, like pins and needles on the skin. There was this light so bright, I walked into that light. The walk continues, for Master Peter can see me as I stand holding Rosie, Gemma's doll, I continue to walk, but my search comes to an end. Wait on the fringes for the return of my baby Gemma. The outpouring of love that I send to you both. Samuel had moved on but we will all unite together very soon. My journey has been long and wearing, trapped in the search. We can all return home soon and make the new life that was meant to be.

The *Titanic* below the ocean should be left be, let the mysteries lie. The sparkle will return, the smile that has long been forbidden will glow like the rainbow you see before you. No longer will Gemma be trapped, Samuel has prepared a simple farm where Gemma can collect eggs from the chickens each morning, a simple life to retreat and repair the damage that has been done to the soul. I return to be with Samuel, to reunite Rosie.

A party frock awaits Gemma, the celebrations to begin. Gratitude and love cannot express for the feeling inside, the ache has gone. There are many in our world who know of that ache. The releasement takes that ache away for many that return. My name has also been engraved on the heart, the heart that is next to the candle.

The pull is great, blessings and eternal love. Goodbye, my friends.

16-04-2021   FRANCIS

Hello, my dears, it's Francis here. No disrespect, I'm just being me. So where do I start? I hope my story will not be too dull for you. Born to my parents, Harold and Cissy, one sister and three brothers, born in Wetherby. Mandy the eldest, the second Barry, then the twins, Tom and Jake.

Mom always said I was dad's favourite – Daddy's girl. For me, dad always looked old; I remember him no other way. His work, steel manufacturing, mauling heavy steel and machine operating. As a child holding hands so rough, yet I felt so safe when large hands cupped mine. My parents, simple but loving. Dad was a good man, father, and husband. Some days his little pleasure, mom would give him a few bob to go to the local with his brothers and brother-in-law. It was known as 'The Pig & Whistle'. All of us would look forward to his return because he was always tipsy; never drunk, but jolly. He would tell stories and bring home packets of crisps and pop, Dandelion & Burdock, my favourite.

I drifted through my school years, I didn't pass my 11 plus but I did O.K. 'O' levels in maths, english and geography. Work, again I would drift. Nothing special, shop work, and working the tills in the local café. I was never ambitious, not like Mandy. Although she was the eldest and a gap between us, we were always close. Clothes were hand-me-downs until that day everything changed.

The curse for dad and he was only forty-five – to me it was a good age, for what did I know, just sixteen. Lung cancer took him. We all thought work had killed him. Not long to follow was mom – that day so vivid in my mind. My eldest brother Barry ran down the stairs shouting, 'Mandy! Mandy! Wendy!' For Mandy's friend was there. 'Mom won't wake up and she's cold to the touch.' We had noticed days before mom was vague; it was cancer of the brain. Mandy was twenty-one, Barry nineteen, and the twins seventeen.

Close-knit we were, all working. It was for Mandy and Barry to take control, to pool the money together, for what did we know of running a home? Life was to change for us all. Uncle Tom visited regularly to see if we were ok. How quick normality took over for life to continue.

A big change for me. My 17th birthday, a group of boys came into the café, they were loud and boisterous. The one that was always smiling shouted over, 'Hey, darling, what's your name?' I neatly replied, 'Francis.' On leaving, he said, 'Give me your phone number and I'll call you.' I replied, 'We don't have such luxuries.' He laughed and said, 'Give me a piece of paper' and he wrote down his name and number. He pushed it into the palm of my hand and clenched my hand into a fist. He winked at me and was gone, I felt my face blush with heat.

Life was too busy to think of boys, for work didn't stop. Cooking and ironing each morning before work, prepare the fire, for winters are hard. November 2nd

that day the cheeky confident boy came into my life. A week had gone by and I had not plucked up the courage to call. Another week went by, the café door opened and in entered this dashing boy. Hairstyle, it reminded me of Elvis. 'If you're not going to ring me,' he said, 'write down your address and I'll pick you up tonight at seven. We can go to the flicks.' Again I felt heat in my face, which made him laugh. It felt like a volcano erupting.

Two years had passed and Barry moved on. His girlfriend was in the family way; he went to live with her parents. The twins were dating. Mandy, I have never known her to have a boyfriend.

On my 18th birthday Paul presented me with a ring. Immediately I felt the presence of a huge hand take mine and the rough skin. I heard those words from dad's voice say, 'Yes, lass, once in lifetime, precious moments.'

Paul was ambitious, the opposite of me. Five years we were engaged.

Childhood, we were such a poor family, but so loving. Paul, of course, passed his 11-plus and went to grammar school. He had a business head. His friend James was to be best man at our wedding. They plotted an idea between them. James was hands-on, a practical lad. They set up a small business. Renting out a garage, they manufactured sheds. Paul was the businessman. Together they would take sheds and assemble them. It grew so fast, cheap and cheerful. As it grew, the quality grew too. They took on two lads fresh from school. The business grew and it grew.

Paul couldn't understand why I continued to work. I became the manager of my own café. Children never came along for us.

Mandy remained in the family home; I had moved on to Thornby. Paul and I drifted on, we discussed adoption. The twist was around the corner, for the speed of the curse that lay dormant for all those years. Paul was sick – a stomach bug he was told. Sickness then blood. November 18th, I was preparing breakfast, I heard a loud thud. 'Paul,' I called, 'are you ok?' I found him on the bathroom floor. The postmortem revealed a large tumour pressing to cause a burst in his stomach. How I wanted to see that month disappear.

Mandy became ill – a shadow of her former self, skin and bone, cancer of the bowel. Mandy had a child, one we could not have. Julie was thirteen and she became my daughter, for Julie and I were always close. It was second nature for Julie to call me mom; so much sadness when families go through so much grief.

With the knowledge that dad was always there, with large rough hands to support me, I was happy. For my daughter gave me such joy. She came to work in the café. 'Mom, let me take over, you're always so tired these days. Stay at home to look after Rex.' (Our Cocker Spaniel) I'd even become too weary to take him for walks. Tests followed but I didn't despair, for Julie was a grown lady, very capable. She was ambitious; she followed her mother, Mandy. I reassured her and told her I would hold her hand just as Dad holds mine.

Always know your loved ones are near. My gift to you both a simple gift, a cup of expresso coffee with a smiling face on top. There is no sorrow, no sadness, only love, respect, and happiness, work, rest, and play in our world. For all the challenges that life throws at you, know that all will be well. Master Peter was chosen for times like this, to hold together the emotions. Where times were emotional, I let tears flow. I felt his struggle, his eyes moist, strength is there.

My thanks for allowing me to share my story and let you know your loved ones are always close. Love is. I say goodbye.

14-05-2021   GORDON

Hello, my friends, I am Gordon.

You are not aware of the joy and laughter of the children. As they play and share jokes, they do brighten my heart.

My story hopefully you learn from. I was born and bred in Northumberland, a modest terraced home, born and to die in that little home. We were what you would call an average family, mom and dad both worked. I followed in dad's footsteps; he would call me a clerk. A stationery company – invoices, audits, checking stock.

As a child I was quiet and timid, school was non-eventful. A target to bully, and that didn't change in adult life. Dad passed suddenly without warning, his heart gave way, fifty-seven years of age – no age at all. Mom fared much better – 88 years old. It was at that time they weren't called carers, but now as I look at it, I was mom's carer. I didn't attend church, but I would put my hand on the bible every day and thank God for every breath that filled my lungs. I guess I got it from mom; she would sit and read the bible over and over. I would try to entice her to read other things, more light-hearted, *Women's Own* magazines. They would sit idle – that was mom. How foolish of me to try and change her.

My favourite hobby, stamp collecting. I had album after album. On the passing of Mom, things changed very little, for the home never saw light, the curtains remained closed. The only visitors were the insurance man, the baker, and the milkman. To me it was natural to sit in the dark, my lamp to highlight the stamps as I browsed through. They gave me such joy, but I see now this was such folly.

The joy the children bring does not compare. A question I kept asking upon my return: what was the purpose of my life? To be invisible? To all around to be labelled a loner and a weirdo? The freedom of the mind in our world, it brings such joy.

The entrapment on earth does not compare. For me to share with you, your troubles on earth, they seem great for so many. For the awakening of the soul and its blossoming in our world is a blessing to behold.

For those that return, the awakening cannot be described in words. So, what was the purpose of my life? To be a foundation for mom and dad, how they tried for many years to conceive. I thought I was a disappointment to them. How wrong I was, just to be was my purpose, so they could lavish love, which they did in bucketloads. I wonder how both of them found it so easy to cry yet I could not shed a tear.

I shared my life in that little terraced house with mom and dad in our world. No curtains, no glass, just sun with rays that shine through lightning up every room. It matters not that it is plain and simple.

I'm privileged to observe the passing of souls, to observe each soul before and after. To see the dark evaporate, the transformation again is beyond words. Each soul is dark when enters but shines brightly upon return.

Continue to send healing and love to Mother Earth.

Many require healing. Toxins evaporate when healing is dispersed. Little did I realise I sent out healing every day when I placed my hand on the bible. My prayers never included myself; I would ask the Lord to help those in need and those in sickness. Little did I know of energies at that time. Little did I know the love a child brings.

My message is brief, but it has purpose. Only now I know upon this return of the heaviness, so I too have gained knowledge from this return. I leave you with an image in your mind of the children in the playground. In the playground, rainbows are used as slides. The joy it brings and the light that penetrates, allowing the souls to return.

My blessings, my thanks. Goodbye, my friends. I shall not return.

11-06-2021   IDA

Welcome, I am Ida. So easy for me to return, the energies of earth just a distance away. Coventry cemetery, let me explain. Like a sensation of pins and needles, all around and voices from all directions. Voices of loved ones, as though drifting on a cloud; voices stronger and stronger as I felt earth's energies drawing from me. Standing there was my loved ones.

Dorothy, my daughter, parents, and grandparents – last of a close family. Dorothy should have visited my grave, but she was there waiting for me, gone before. The transformation so light, the energies, Dorothy stood there so full of colour. She was a strange girl. She breezed through school, she never brought any friends home, never played like other children. She would sit at home and read – not children's books, but my books, Mills and Boon. Her life, she was born in Wolverhampton. Before she was one, her father left. I had no choice but to live with my parents, her home for the rest of her life. Her adult life she worked part time in an office. In her free time, she volunteered to work with children with learning difficulties. They went out on trips, she was happy and contented. In the evenings she would knit, knit for England, winter cardigans, she would darn socks and crochet. She was very gifted, unlike myself. She was not one for new clothes. Time and time again I would say, 'Buy a bright headscarf.' Her dress was very dowdy. It was her way, she was happy and content.

No friends, no boyfriends. The time came when I stopped worrying, years passed, and I assumed she would look after me in my old age. What did I want? I had a loving daughter, she was caring and would cook, clean, etc. But she drew the line at gardening. I loved to potter in the garden. Tell me, how can a person have no friends and no social life? 'Mom, my social life, is the children who cling to my hands. I feel their love as we walk together on school trips. They gaze up at me and feel protected.'

The long curse, the plague that took her grandad and so many on earth. It took just weeks from the diagnosis. She looked unwell, with tinges of yellow around the eyes. Cancer of the liver and it was advanced. Year after year I would visit Dorothy's grave with a rose. I would sit there and talk to her, not knowing that she was not there. I had no belief, no religion, no belief in eternal life. My search ended on that day. The pins and needles, the voices so clear.

I come through this day with a headscarf full of colour. Dorothy placed it on me, upon my arrival. I used to joke to my friend Sonja,' I'm going to visit the boneyard today!'

The flame burns so brightly; not all souls are trapped, those like I were searching. It was my wish to be laid with loved ones, there are many that do the same. There are times when a trapped soul is there for a reason; it's not a punishment but a choice of the soul. There are times, no matter how hard a healer tries, a soul can resist. Questions... I asked of Dorothy, only now do

I understand. I would ask, 'Why did you lead the life you did? I was very sociable and so was your father, for all of his bad traits.' I now understand what the eyes see sometimes is falseness. Judgement is an earthly thing.

At this moment in time, I feel more comfortable in this earth as the energies are so light in our world. Yes, I will convalesce but not until I visit the cemetery once more. It is not a myth to have as you wish in this world: think it and it is there! There is time for work and time for play. The physical body has no interest, the mind can see. Do you rely on sight or an image in your mind? Close your eyes and see those images. It is no different in this world. Can you see, hear, smell, and touch? The senses remain, you have choices to use how you wish. Part of my convalescence, a plain bed in a plain room with a bookcase, and why not Mills and Boon? Familiarities of earth make transgression easier. I have no wish to return, all my family are here.

I leave you a single rose to leave on your wooden heart in the centre of the table where you sit. One of you to draw a rose, permission is asked of Anthony and Wendy; a rose with no thorns. I must return now. Acknowledge that I stand at the head of the circle. Be aware the energy so powerful, my dear friends.

God's love with you both, and the pins and needles have started. Farewell.

25-06-2021   HILDA

Welcome, Master Peter and Lady Ann. It is I, Hilda.

A local lass, Small Heath born and bred, one of six – me being the eldest; seven if you include Jack, our dog. Dad used to joke, 'He is a cross between a Great Dane and a Romany.' A big black dog, he would wander but always return. Life was simple but hard. At the age of thirteen I was skilled in cooking, sewing, darning, and ironing. I was like a mother to my brothers and sisters. William was just a year younger. I would push him to the coal yard in our wheelbarrow. My education was sparse. The radio would crackle and groan as mother & father sat there intently. The war was looming. In our world now, I still recall the sirens, the pitch black, and the quietness.

My father built the air raid shelter that my mother was reluctant to use because it was damp and would flood. Those times, my mother would gather us all together in the kitchen. It was the easiest escape route, she would say. Mother would try, and I would try, to keep us all together – four, seven, and nine years old. Very exciting times for us children. Many homes were destroyed and they became our playgrounds.

My father worked at the railway; his knowledge was with freight. His brother Ted was never to return from the war. Uncle Ted once said to me, 'Listen to your mother and father, always be respectful. Have that attitude through life, lass, as you grow.' The scars of those years remain, families torn apart. Only William and I remained at home, the others shipped out to the countryside. As a female, I was too valuable to be sent away.

Growing up, mother and father always made Sunday special – not for religion. Sunday was the day for families. Father always wore a crisp ironed shirt with collars. Those were the days when the joint he would carve, simple memories that the war would deprive. So many unmarked graves. It is of no importance now, my remains lie in Yardley cemetery, it is unmarked and overgrown, on the south side under the pine. It's of little importance, for only now do I understand.

I am not new to your dwelling, for Francis knew of me and the little inn you call The White Swan, Brown ale my father would drink there. The fields were green and lush, the trees were plenty. The small parish church, and I recall the day of the jumble sale. The wooden floor, I would tap and pretend I could dance. The dwellings were sparse on your lane. I have sat where others have sat in your dwelling.

Master Dennis, (Mr Dennis was the previous owner of Sunrise) sense those energies, for they return to gaze out. Take away your laurels and gaze out and see the farm in the distance, with streams that ran and meadows with wildflowers. For hours on end, I would sit and watch the trains go by. Be aware of the energies, be aware of the children as they flourish and play. I was never one to complain. Respect all life, animal and human.

Crohn's disease took me. I was not one for religion, I was not one to ask or pray. Life was simple, 'Take life in your stride lass,' Uncle Ted would say. It is not always those you expect upon your return to meet you. For William was so close, he too was taken. We didn't know he had a weak heart as a child, barely into adulthood. I would talk to him for years and years, unaware that he could hear me. On my return it was Uncle Ted that was waiting. 'Lass,' he always called me, 'William will come when you are ready.' What did this mean? 'The adjustment is not complete,' he said, 'only when the adjustment is complete.' Understand that there is this adjustment, and each individual adjusts differently. Although no time, there is still time. Time is so different from what you know.

My purpose of this visit is for you to be aware of the energies of your little dwelling. When that time comes, which it will, you will not see in your lifetime or in families after. Time will come when the dwelling will only exist in our world.

The pull is great, respect as always, my fondest farewells.

30-07-2021 LOUISE

Welcome, Lady Ann and Master Peter. I thank you for this time I spend with you.

Introductions first. I am Louise. My family that I leave behind, that I view regularly – husband Brian, son David, and daughter Samantha. Formalities over, please call me Lou. That's how I was known. My husband Brian, son Davey, not forgetting Sammy. Why not mention them, as I watch them grow and unfold as a beautiful flower? It starts off as a stem, and a petal slowly but surely opens, and its prime and beauty shines out to the world. The time will come when the petals fade and wither around the edges, as time slowly draws to an end.

My beautiful Sammy, soon to give birth to a beautiful girl, to a gorgeous little girl. She will also be athletic and sporty like her mother, grandmother, grandad, and uncle. As a family we were very outgoing and very sporty. David played football and Sammy netball. We would travel to Wales and Cornwall. The bikes would go where we go – mountain trekking too, cross track through the woods and only the best bikes would do.

It was said that my family and I were fitness fanatics, to be healthy and to feel good about yourself. Not only physical, but mentally also. So, I watch them develop. Davey will not be a parent – he has no interest – but what a wonderful uncle he will be. My Brian and Davey remain very close – days together, holidays together, cycling and running.

Davey tries hard to take his dad out of the situation, the guilt he carries forward, the formality of the consent form. He feels he has signed away my life. It all began, irregular periods. High blood pressure, visits to the gynaecologist and so on, and so the journey goes on. Scans revealed as we sat in that office opposite the consultant, Brian squeezing my hand so tight. Those words were like a knockout punch, the word tumour with small tumours attached. 'Pack your bag, Mrs Jones, we need to operate as soon as possible.' Pull no punches, a 50-50 chance of survival. I was in a daze for days; that feeling continues to this day.

Children are resilient, for Davey and Sammy to never forget. They both move on with their lives, not like their dad, stuck in treacle and guilt. Embrace your life, embrace the sad times as well as the happy. We had busy hectic lives, we had a life of fun and laughter, we were the family that were 'go-getters', we were a social family that all wanted to be with. It pleases me that Davey and Sammy follow that trend.

Now, to that day, It was all a daze, so what do I recall? The operation is going well, alright. I could hear voices all around, the voices got louder and louder. I still hear that voice as she cried out, 'We are losing her!' For me, it was a dream. My hand was held tight. 'Who are you?' I asked. She smiled; she was so serene and calming, there was a glow about her. I felt a tug and a release. We were walking in countryside as she held my hand. So green, fields so green, trees so tall, branches leaned towards me as if saying, 'Hello, welcome to our world.' I felt at peace, a peace I have never known, and I get a little sad as I tell you this, this is my experience. It differs greatly for others. Other factors come into play, major factors.

My passing was wonderful. 'Who are you?' She just smiled, with no reply. I can tell you now she was the lady of the light. The lady of the light still travels with me everywhere. The connection, when we travel; to hold hands, and the connection is always there. Just as Brian held my hand so firm that day. When the time is right my husband will hold my hand again. We will travel and observe and watch over our grandchild as she grows.

Davey and I so look forward to his wedding day. Tradition counts for nothing, for we are a family that did things our way. His dad will walk down the aisle with the bride, also the best man. Upon so close a bond, so close father and son, it's the way it was. Sammy and I were close. I know she is aware, for when I visit she looks round. 'Mum, I love you. I know you are here and our daughter will know all about you also.'

Samantha's daughter Charlotte, before she is three years old she will have a hand-built canoe. Prams and dolls will not exist. Yes, a tomboy, but what a beautiful girl she will grow into. Acknowledge the fact that you can view your family that you have left behind. You can touch them with your thoughts, with your smell, and your energy.

So much time I spend with Brian. He did not let guilt affect his work, proficient is what he does. The only time that he is competitive is when Davey runs with him, canoes and cycles with him. Davey made a pledge before the operation, 'Mum, I'll look after Dad.' It has been said many times, you have choices on earth and choices in our world. My choice is to be close to my family to support Brian in every way possible. Until that day that grip returns, then and only then will the guilt disappear.

There is no blame on the surgeon; the post-mortem revealed a weakness of the heart. This would have manifested in middle age. The warning signs would've shown much earlier if I hadn't have been so fit. I was only thirty-three years of age.

Time moves on, for other family members have returned home since. We will rejoice on the birth of Charlotte, how quickly Samantha bounces back. My message to you: do not be fearful, they are always there and their touch can be felt. My passing was beautiful, move on. The lady of the light will soon move on. Yet to occur, my dear husband will develop a cough. Yes he will, he will neglect it no matter what David says. The struggle to keep up, as he lags behind with the running. The loss to both, but yet again David will move on with his life. So there it is, that was us as a family.

I thank you for this time, to let you know that your loved ones are always there. Fear not, for passing is a beautiful thing. I can only speak of my experience. I did not look down and see myself in the operating theatre. Others may have – not I, just the grip and the peace. That tug removed me from the table and theatre to a world of beauty.

It has been a blessing for me. This has been a blessing, a privilege not only to talk to you but to watch those souls as peace engulfs them as they pass. They too feel serene love, a privilege to see. Those that have communicated before also observe as I, beauty the human mind cannot comprehend.

Thank you, Lady Ann, Master Peter, and all those that sit with you.

Farewell.

13-08-2021 JOAN

Hello, my dears, it is I, Joan.

Back in those days when it was far, far slower than today – your life is hectic – a beautiful part of your world, Lytham Saint Annes, is where I shared my life with my husband Eric, a sweet gentleman. He was content with his own company, but not I , to be with me is to chat all day!

Many years of my life involved with the local post office and sweet shop. So diverse was each day, so many generations to converse with. Pension day, or the day for young mothers to collect their 'child allowance'. Weekends, when children with their pocket money would visit. How different they were – some clever and spent wisely, half penny here, a penny there, to get as much as possible; where others, their eyes would bulge and they would have one or two items only.

I did enjoy my life. There were times when the mothers would say, 'Joan, how do you do it? You always seem so happy with your husband!' We went on long walks hand-in-hand, and not forgetting Skip, a loyal companion, a Cocker Spaniel. My reply was always the same, 'I always enjoy Eric's company, and I look for the positives in our relationship, never the negatives.' Mothers would say to me, 'If only it were that simple Joan'. My reply, 'Life is as simple or as complicated as you make it.'

Our life was simple – a house, a townhouse, a small car, a Morris Minor. A little runabout, it also became part of our little family, and oh, as the years rolled by it never let us down. We never travelled far. Many offered to buy our little car when they saw the low mileage. My reply, 'Is it good or bad to have low mileage?' In our lives we cover so much. My personal life went round the clock many times; if I were a car, I would have over half a million miles on my clock.

Although I did not travel far, the conversations were many. Let me tell you, it's not always the old that are wise. There were many times when I would say to a parent, 'That very young child of yours has a very wise head on young shoulders.' 'I don't know where they would get that from, not me or their dad,' they would say. I would say to them. 'Maybe they have been here before.' 'Oh Joan, do you really believe that? You only live once,' they would say. My reply, 'If that is the case, then live a good life!'

I have learnt so much from Eric. I would tell them he is gentle and sweet. He never got angry as Skip ran after squirrels, much to my annoyance. 'Be gentle with him, Joan,' he would say. Skip would lie in front of the fire and rest his feet on Eric's slippers. I would say, 'It's the softness of your slippers.' 'He's showing his love,' Eric would say.

In later years, Eric spent his time reading cowboy books. He had a love of John Wayne and Audey Murphy. As my love, my work, that was his love, and our long walks together. He would say to me, 'You know, Joan, you never discuss your work. I respect that, because I know mother's and grandmother's confide in you.' They do, I would tell them what is in my heart; my reply always comes from the heart.

I have chosen to return very soon. The map has been drawn, each hurdle has been shown. Let me be clear, my dears, you have to give your consent to the life you return to. Again, you have choice to return. My life will be so different; at that point of conception the slate will be wiped clean. What would be the point of a life you already knew? Where would the purpose and drive be? The life I will leave behind, just a part of my life in this world, was to ease the passing of those that returned. On earth I could talk, talk and talk, so many were so grateful. To talk to those upon their return, for gentleness and love second nature to me.

What are the parts of my life in this world? The bridge between one culture and another. It was like I had a welding rod in my hand, and to weld the seam was invisible. To knit one culture to another was so easy for me, and they are the gifts I brought back to this world. They are an asset, but again you have choice. You may wish to have a simple life, where you tend the garden and never venture elsewhere. That is the minority in this world, they are not frowned upon. There is a level playing field but most wish to serve.

I will give you only a slight insight into my new life, I should not be more important than the other. There are those that can wield power, power for the good. That was one of the conditions, for you are allowed conditions upon your return. It was so, so tempting on my return to have a little post office and dwindle my time away, but then I would waste all that I had learned. In our simple dwelling in this world, we also have Skip by our side. My dears, I say to you, enjoy all generations whatever limitations the body has, physical or mental.

Yes, children bring joy, but a child becomes old one day. It is a sad fact on earth some of the elderly are cast aside. That time will come on your earth where there is a level playing field. That is the goal, my dears. My message is simple, respect all ages, speak from the heart, be diverse.

Eric and I had no children, it never happened. We didn't question, we just accepted. I had a huge family to watch – young mothers became grandmothers; the young children who spent their pocket money, to watch them become mothers; their mothers before them also confided in me. One in particular made me smile, 'Joan,' she said, 'your hair was long when I was a child. I was mesmerised by the colour and length.' The length had not changed, only the colour – silver grey, I did laugh.

It was so sad, that sweet little girl, a young mother, she was taken in her prime. At her funeral Eric said, 'Don't be sad, Joan. She gave you pleasure as she grew, as you gave her pleasure.' On my return, I realised the wisdom that Eric spoke. Surely that little girl and young mother was standing side-by-side with Eric. The joy of seeing them both on my return was a love I've never felt before. I didn't think it was possible to feel a love so intense. My love, my life on earth in that little post office was complete.

There are times, my dears, you just have to listen. Like a Morris Minor, the tyres to be replaced, and miles roll on and on. Look at your life, when those tyres are replaced you return to our world, and the miles roll on and on. Be good, be gentle, be kind, and hope that many, many souls pass this day.

I give their thanks as they pay their respects in their own way.

Goodbye, my dears.

10-12-2021   BARRY Re: BARBARA

Hello, my sweethearts, I come with much love and sincerity. I was christened Barry but please address me as Barbara.

I was born in Sunderland, Low Street. My father was a clever man, a technical engineer. My mother, my sweet, sweet mother, was a music teacher. My adorable sister Margaret. There you have my family, a family with a big question mark. From an early age I was so different, a massive disappointment to my father. Such an unhappy child, from the age of four years I saw several psychiatrists. Schooling was awful; bullying, but only to go home and the bullying to continue. 'You disappoint me, son,' he would say. 'Why can't you be more like your sister?' Margaret loved school and excelled at sports and exams. Education passed me by. How can you learn when you're so unhappy? Trapped in a body that does not fit? The picture is not complete; you cannot force a jigsaw piece to fit with another or disappointment will follow. My father stood six feet tall, Margaret stood six feet tall. I loathed to be so tall, I didn't fit! How I longed to be small and petite.

My sweet, sweet mother took me out of school, one after the other. The time came when she left her post as a music teacher and educated me at home. I was then fourteen years old and in hell. My saviour came – a lady counsellor, following a long, long list.

Master Peter, this will bring memories to you. For Eve, the counsellor, spoke of her family and her daughter, son, and husband, also her hobbies. I would sit and listen and think, why isn't she asking me questions? The turmoil I'm going through. The therapy, so simple, yet to open the dam inside of me to allow the waters to flow. My saviour until the day of my death. On her birthday and Christmas, flowers and cards, forever a friend, so well thought of. The time came when it was almost impossible to see her, but I would visit her home. Her family were very understanding. She asked permission to speak to my father, only then did the abuse stop.

Two days after my 16th birthday, I left home. My father said to my mother, 'He's gone to join the other freaks.' We were like a little tribe, moving from one abandoned building to another. In that tribe, another saviour came along – Liam, who was christened Litta. So now you see the puzzle come together. Our minds knew what each other was going through, the support we had for each other was immense. We both underwent hormone treatment and operations. We found ourselves to fit; by the ignorant we were seen as the odd couple. Those who took the time to know us became lifelong friends, particularly the females, they felt so safe with us.

As I was moving from one building to another I would paint landscapes. I had compliments on my work. With my knowledge, Liam took one of them to an art shop. It was sold the next day, and that's how it continued. I became an artist and Liam had his skills – he worked sewing clothes. We both found work; no longer dropouts, we both contributed to society. We scrimped and saved and bought a two-bedroom semi in Durham – far enough away, but close enough to see my mother and sister. But only on the understanding that they never spoke of me to my father.

From that day as a sixteen-year-old, I never saw or spoke to my father again, and he never mentioned me either. My mother continued her career as a music teacher. Margaret went on to become a nurse, so dedicated, to become a Sister, she was highly thought of.

It was a sad day when she passed of cancer. I asked my mother if Margaret could be buried. Selfish of me, it was so I could visit and talk to her. I always had this belief that she could hear me from the grave.

Please understand the difficulties to be born in the wrong body. People were so ignorant. We are no different; we have so much compassion and love. It was not fitting that my mother should lose both of us before her passing. I became unwell, a cough that would not budge, cancer also. Liam and my mother, one each side of the bed, both hands held tightly. Liam now wears both rings. He still resides in the little semi in Durham. The orders are few, which suites him fine for his fingers are not nimble.

My sweeties, on your journeys through your lives, if someone does not fit your hand like a snug glove, do not berate them, do not shun them. Greet them with open arms, for they have a greater understanding of love than you will ever know.

The adjustment to this world was so easy, the love so familiar. For I held both their hands and they were tailor-made to fit. Remember, my darlings, whatever the ailment, however odd one seems, make that special effort to make them feel whole.

My blessings on each of you. I will return at some stage and let you know what progress I make in this world with Liam by my side.

Farewell.

07-01-2022   ABIGAIL

Hello, my lovelies, I am Abigail, born and reared in north west London, Edgware. I come in this day with my sister Jane. We were inseparable in our time on earth. Our home, a modest four-bedroom detached. My mother had little ambition, her school days and everything in fact came easy, lack of ambition, qualifications meant nothing. My father was very ambitious, a qualified accountant, lead accountant of a joinery and kitchen company. That was where my mother and father met, my mother was a typist. They soon became a partnership, and to the dismay of both parents my mother became pregnant with Jane, and I was to follow eighteen months later. Not until we both left home did she resume her career; our childhood was a break for her.

Jane and I were so close. One memory locked in my brain: I was seven years old, Jane eight, it was Christmas Day, we each had a nurse's uniform. How we loved those uniforms – that was to become a major part of our lives. School was easy for both of us, we both passed our 11+, and we both went to grammar school. Jane followed mother, little ambition and lacking confidence. Although older, Jane looked to me to guide her and give her confidence. We played together and, to the dismay of boyfriends, we were also in a foursome.

Qualifications easy to obtain, Jane would not go to nursing college on her own. To the upset of our parents, she spent one year working in a supermarket. The day arrived, we both left home on the same day.

Northampton Nursing College – some would say training school, to us a nursing college. Degrees again came easy. We eventually worked in Salisbury Hospital. We loved our work, it was like being set free. Mother was all for letting us go, but father always worried about his girls. Oh, we so let our hair down at nursing college.

Jane was happy to stay as she was, as she had little ambition. I was very ambitious and went on to run wards. The military would have been so proud of my wards, they ran so well. There was little time in our lives for men, we were dedicated to our careers. In time, things changed and Jane met her future husband. He was quite happy to go out with two of us, and vice versa. We settled in Salisbury, we loved that area – a little town called Redlynch.

There was a parting in our working lives, two opposites: Jane to work with the young, and I the old. Jane became a midwife, and I went on to work at Salisbury Hospice. The change was so rewarding for us both. We each had two sons – Arthur and Reginald, and my sons were James and Andrew. Although we were close, Jane always dressed old-fashioned; she always thought I was too outrageous. We often said we should have been born twins because we could read each other's minds.

My dears, never be surprised at what life throws at you, what ironic twists there can be. I was to witness many deaths, and I would sense them all around me. The names would call out to me in my dream state.

I was to enter the hospice as a patient, fellow workers to care for me. I would observe them as tears rolled down their cheeks. My passing was peaceful. The warning came earlier that day – my mother stood there, hardly recognisable, she looked so young. A month after my departure, Jane enrolled at the same hospice. We are both still remembered to this day.

My lovelies, if you are fortunate to have a love so strong as Jane and I, that love becomes stronger in our world. We travel together, we work together. It goes without saying, we work with the old and the young. Each individual has their own little sanctuary, for time the soul to heal in their own energies.

Farewell.

21-01-2022   RAYMOND

Welcome, firstly, I must introduce myself, for my mom always taught us to be polite, Raymond is my name. I was born and bred in a small village – Borden, near Maidstone. We lived in a row of cottages, council-owned. I was one of ten – four brothers and five sisters. We were known locally as a 'rough' family, yet we were always polite. Perhaps it was our attire, as we were not the most polished children in the neighbourhood. It wasn't until my late teens when I was to wear new clothing. It was just accepted to wear hand-me-downs; it was natural. There were some of us that had trouble walking from shoes that didn't fit or worn against our stride.

Our home was simple – a large back garden, where freight trains used to pass by. The garden was my paradise. Dad grew vegetables, and that became my love. We only saw dad at weekends; he was a miner and would travel with four other men in a lorry, sharing travel and accommodation expenses. Ah yes… We must have all been conceived at weekends. Absence makes the heart grow fonder, so they say. I do think, looking back, it kept mom and dad close.

I would work in the garden with dad. 'Son,' he would say, 'play with your brothers and sisters.' I had no interest, only Celia I was close to. We were ten months apart. How she hated that name – she was always called Cissy, which she was happy with. I remember so well when dad said I could have my own part of the garden to grow what I wished. I collected blue bricks, piled at the bottom of the garden. I pretended to be a bricklayer and placed them on top of each other. I put blue clear plastic on the top and they were my cold frames, I did think I was clever.

School was a labour for me, not the brightest button in the class. The times I was dragged there by my mom. There were so many days I would go missing. I walked amongst the orchards. My dad would say, 'So much for you to do, go play with the others.' He knew deep down that I was happy to play and work in the garden. As the years rolled by, of course I became a gardener.

My brothers and sisters left home one by one, some to get married, some to start their careers. Two brothers left, never to be heard of again. Although mom was hurting, she hid it well. 'It's their choice,' she would say. I always remained close to Cissy, my sister, my only friend, I was what you would call a loner.

The years rolled on, and there was only mom and me. mom's life was so sheltered, her life was cooking, washing, and cleaning. No ambition. I don't believe she travelled further than Maidstone. She became a member of the local church; this gave her great satisfaction. She would help at jumble sales at the local hall. There was a stall that sold vegetables only. With permission from the council and donations for the church, I applied for a stall at the local council market for a weekend selling vegetables. This was short lived because the council stepped in. Although they were from my garden, it was classed as 'council property'.

Cissy was married to an estate agent, where she worked part time. She also raised a son, Ronny. One day she called round so excited. 'Raymond,' she said, 'there is a plot of land, just under three acres, and it has just come up for sale. We could purchase it between the three of us.' To me £900 was a great sum of money. In no time at all, the land was sown and glass houses were built. For two long years of hard slog, we toiled. Cissy had a business head, not like me. We were to sell vegetables direct, wholesale. It was a trickle at first, then a stream, which became a river.

Cissy's husband was all for expanding the business, I was not. I was happy with my lot, to pay my way, a simple man with a simple life. I remained in the cottage where I was born and where I was to die. There was a bitter divorce between Cissy and her husband, it was caused by greed. Against Cissy's wishes, I financed part of the business to pay him off. How this went against him, for Ronnie, his son, disowned him.

Ronnie was so like his mom. He loved to be in the garden of my home. 'Let me help you, Uncle Raymond.' I had arthritis in my fingers. He would turn up with school friends. One day he came with the handle of a spade, he had chiselled the end to a point. 'Uncle, I'll make the holes and you plant the seed.' I believe he was planting seeds in his own mind; I was of no use with crippled hands. Cissy continued with the business, and Ronnie was her right-hand man.

It was my wish that upon my death, my savings went to the church as it gave mom so much pleasure. To those looking on from the outside would think my life was mundane. I had no wish to travel; my love, my passion, was the garden, the soil. I was so rich with contentment, my friends. If you have a love, a passion so great, you will succeed. Inner peace, contentment, enrichment is all you require.

My dad had so many children, yet his eyes never set on a grandchild, and there were many. We were told complications of the chest. He was a young man still in his 30s, mom was to fare better. One of my duties in the winter months was to cook the porridge and let it soak overnight. How mom loved her porridge in the winter months. A cold December morning, mom was sitting where she always sat doing her knitting. She looked so peaceful, just shy of her 88th birthday. She was a New Year's Day baby. She was buried with dad, that was her wish. My wish was that my ashes would be scattered amongst my vegetables, that was the instructions for Ronnie.

My friends, if you are lucky enough to find a passion, a love that gives you contentment, you have found riches beyond words.

A thought for you all: There are those that lie beneath your oceans in ships and submarines. They have become their graves; they will not leave the vessel behind. Those of our world who are dedicated to healing enter those vessels, for the souls are content to remain. It is their choice for the brothers to unite in their physical death, a bond formed they will not break. It is their wish to lie beneath the oceans in our world. Yet again we stress, not all those lost souls wish to return. They are not trapped. Earth has a greater pull for them, they do not idle. Some are souls you can refer to as 'Earth angels'.

The next visit, we will change strategy and Anoku to talk of future events on your earth. Just a little insight to feed the mind. Before I leave you, the night before mom came to visit in my dreams. I remember those words so well: 'I'm coming to bring you home, Raymond.' The next night, on going to bed I didn't wake up again.

It was fitting that Ronnie found me. His words echoed on my return. 'Uncle Raymond looked so peaceful.' nan would say, 'God bless you.' God bless you all, farewell.

18-03-2022   ANOKU, AXL

Welcome followers, Anoku here. It is not for me to know who will speak this day.

First, I will clear up a little misunderstanding. Those that cause atrocities on your earth. A beautiful garden with fragrance and flowers of every description, animals and insects, awaits them. A serene garden full of love at every turn, that is a progression. The extent of the atrocities, the dense darkness and, yes, the Seeth, play a big part. Yes, there is darkness, as the density fades and the dark becomes grey, the shades of grey become light.

The entrance to the garden was always there. It becomes clear, but not all venture out immediately. If you recall Walker, the hitman, the reluctance to cross that bridge for all those atrocities. They carry one common goal – fear within. If I return this quarter is not clear. My farewell, good day, fellow healers.

AXL

I join you as your sun shines so brightly, we hear your laughter. Now we talk of the soul, but first allow me to introduce myself: I am called Axl, I am told I am wise. What does that mean in our world? I work on a higher plane than Anoku. What is the soul? The soul is the life force for all eternity that cannot, I emphasise CANNOT, be destroyed. The soul enters the keeper, and the keeper has free reign. The soul cannot interfere; the keeper makes the decisions to work with love or to commit atrocities. In your world, who is to say what is right or wrong?

Who gives that right to punish? Your world is so corrupt. To a degree, you are told untruths, what you would call 'brainwashed'. The keeper that is true to themselves works in pure love. It would be wrong of me to guide you as to what is the right or wrong way. Remember that soul learns from those atrocities.

Let us talk of healing, there is a gradual process from the dark into the beautiful garden. It is for I and those who work as I do to decide on the return of each soul and the healing that is required.

First, we will talk of the keeper who has a natural death. Old age will fit the description, their healing is minimal. It has been said before they find themselves in a plain building, there are walls but no ceiling, they lie on a plain bed. In their time, and their time only, there is the splendour of the garden. The aroma of the flowers, the freshness of the grass, arouses all the senses. In no time, they return to a home they wish.

We will talk on the human body where death occurs by drowning. It matters, does the keeper drown in sea water, river, or soap water. Are the waters warm or cold? Salt affects the soul differently from river water, lake, or soap water. Each is taken into consideration of which area of the soul to heal.

The soul is very complex, if you think of the human brain, the complexity of the soul is one thousand times more complex. In your world there is a saying, and again only to a degree it is true, 'healing is healing'. But it is the intent that is of great importance. Each one of you that sit here this day bring different qualities. On your return you have a choice to use those qualities. Each one of you would not heal the same part of the soul.

If the keeper suffers loss of life through fire, was the keeper burnt almost immediately or was the known cause smoke, or was there an explosion to damage the human body? There is great importance as to how the keeper passes to our world. What was the cause?

If a keeper suffers from a disease – a slow, slow process – there are specialised healers for each part of the soul. It is not random. On the return it is for I and others to assess the damage to the soul. One may require one healer; others may require several to work on them. Only those that pass with natural causes come to our world to rest.

When the aroma of the beautiful garden reaches them, it is then their journey begins. They sit and review their life. Before they continue their work, they have a very important decision to make. Do they return? If they choose not to return, their qualities are taken into consideration: where best to serve? Should they choose to return, it is only when they themselves signal that return. If they wish to explore and return to the facet of the diamond, with their family, that is their choice. Knowing they will return in their time, again they have choice.

On that return, gender is of no importance. They may choose to return to heal, where a child was taken before, to feel that love. They may choose a keeper that gives out love from every pore, or a keeper full of hate. So complex is the soul; it adjusts in an instance.

I am a wise one where healing is concerned. Always be aware when you heal, you heal that part of the soul you specialise in. It is not for you to know; it is for you to know your job is done. Fellow healers, it will be I who assess each one of you upon your return. In an instant you will recognise my energy.

Farewell for now.

01-04-2022   ANOKU, JUKA

Welcome friends, Anoku here.

The essence of your world changes, cosmic rays bombard your world. Subtle changes, the viewfinder to your world available to so many. Our world, and yes other worlds that travel, view from afar; their worlds fearful of your world and others. They come in peace but prepare for the hostilities of your world. If you would corner an animal, nine times out of ten it would attack. Left to roam as it pleases, it would be placid. It is wrong to invade and dictate, this is the manner of earth. It is necessary to change so that history does not repeat itself. The cosmic rays, already the reaction to those changes. For man to hold up his hands and gesture no more and stand up in defiance, only then will leaders of your world take note. There is a saying on your world we hear so many times, 'Lessons to be learnt.' But yet from one crisis to another!

Those with a stigma attached – those you would call learning difficulties, the unborn – lessons to be learnt. It is not only the younger generation but the older generation also. Those changes are taking place as we speak. So much talk of ascension and awakening. This has not just begun; it has taken many, many moons on your earth. It has been said the leaders of your world have no choice, people of all quarters will make their voices heard, unity will prevail. This meeting is not for me to answer questions. They will be answered when the time is ripe.

I stand to one side to allow a wiser energy than I.

JUKA

Welcome, friends, Juka here. I attune to your energies.

I will talk in layman's terms. I present you with an elevator, the basement, the dark levels. The first level for those, for adjustment, where acts of evil on mankind were committed. Until that level is complete, the elevator does not move up to the second floor. Let me be clear to you: level one, two, three, and four, and so on, the beauty of our world is amazing. With each level attained, there is greater responsibility and greater knowledge. The higher the level, more avenues open up. Many who returned from your world have returned to level two or three. There are those of you that belong to this small gathering, on your return who will return to level four. You will notice many, many changes. Two of you return to level five, and there is one of you that returns to the level they came from – level eight. And that one has been addressed befitting of that level from which Goddess Aqua resides.

To understand those levels as qualified healers: level three your station; level four allows you unaided to travel to earth, to communicate to bring your love. Previously level three, you travel with higher level beings. That is always the case with the lower levels.

You have on your world what you call spiritualist churches, we would call them spiritualist sanctuaries. It matters not if it were a wooden cabin or humble dwellings under canvas. A spiritual sanctuary where communication takes place. It is said that your channels have guides; those guides are the higher energies. They allow your loved ones to communicate.

To communicate through a higher channel, or to settle on the lower levels – there is always that choice for those that return. On that level, it is as though restraints have been taken away. To travel under your own energy and not to be given permission, the two we have spoken of return to level five. They travel to other worlds, and they gain the knowledge to expand. One will see no change at level eight.

I, Juka, am not a judge. I am, to put it in layman's terms, I am one of your traffic lights. I change those colours, when your soul has acquired the knowledge to climb to a higher level, the next level. To press that button in that elevator. The amber is to give notice to the soul that change is taking place. It is preparation for the soul. Again, the greater the knowledge, the greater the wisdom. Let me tell you, in our world the adjustment is not quick; it is not the blink of an eye from one level to the next. The higher the soul climbs the longer it takes. There are many that do not climb higher than level three, for the soul is content.

We will talk of the Roman soldier who was content in the beautiful garden. Level two, the soul will not rise again, that soul will not return, that soul is content in our world. Each of you, the soul reaches out to different levels, it is not for me to say you have reached contentment level. There is one who sits here this day who will not rest until they reach the high level. I know of this, as I tuned into your energies before I addressed you all. A restless soul that will climb and reach that goal.

I have given Anoku permission to allow you all to ask questions, but not this day as the time is not right. The essence, the energies change as we speak; the magnet pull of those energies the imbalance. I have to take my leave.

Farewell, my friends.

20-05-2022   ANOKU, JACOB

Welcome and greetings, friends.

There are stars you can see with the human eye in your galaxy and those that reach far beyond the human eye, in what you call space centres. Great magnification you cannot view, twin earths, far, far beyond in the great galaxies of life.

In time, man – scientists and engineers – will develop technologies, breakthrough after breakthrough. The stargate… ah, another word bounded around your world… this place where you sit this day and record the channel and the prayer of Lady Ann, it could be known as a stargate.

The exodus of those souls began, search your minds scratching away, a great mine. Mark opened the channel; for him it was like scratching a mine with a nail file. Achievements not to be scoffed at. Is this channel not a stargate? Each world has many stargates, stars in your galaxy, minor and major planets, there will be mass exodus of your world in time.

There is truth, although a little twisted, would that exodus be caused by nature, mankind, or will that exodus be of craft, manmade, or both. There is a fable in your world, Noah's ark and a great wooden ship, the floods. It has been said great ships will travel your skies, deep into your galaxy. The young, the healthy, and the rich, others will follow and the elderly will not be forgotten.

Talk of earth angels, they travel your earth, they walk amongst you unnoticed 99% of the time. Talk of miracles on your earth; earth angels they play their part.

The sun is of great importance, but again the sun is mirrored. This is to allow for that great escape. Would this be the reason each world mirrors itself? Why would earth be the only priority? Life is precious, in bodily form, for all species, all worlds. Each individual serves for one common cause, to put glory on that cause. You can call it the golden age – a label only. Look beyond the label, no matter how grand it may appear.

I am aware of the confusion of the time that I speak of. I will talk on one matter again with permission from Jacob. Yes, I have previously avoided this topic, you would call it skirting around this issue. Without permission from Jacob, I would not say I was one of the perpetrators for the loss of his beloved. Jacob at that time was so full of hate. He moved at stealth under the cover of darkness, he lay low when the sun was full. Titus was the first to be slain. There were suspicions, but not until the second perpetrator was slain. Jacob left his calling card, an arrow above the knee to render helpless. The tour began, both bodies identical, leaving no doubt. I, Anoku, was guarded day and night. Full of remorse and full of guilt, I made my escape under cover of darkness.

Evening came, I walked towards the great sands. I wore flimsy clothing in the knowledge if Jacob didn't find me, I would freeze, so death was guaranteed. On entering the great sands, the wild cries were deafening. The sand creatures cries rang out into the night. Little did I know they were warning Jacob of danger. The cold soon started to take its effect as my walk became slower and slower.

In the distance, through blurred eyesight, a figure stood with bow arched. 'Jacob, I come to you to take my life.' There was hesitation before that arrow struck accurately to the heart centre; death was instant. Peace was overwhelming. On my return, I could not penetrate the dark, as the guilt and remorse remained. A question repeated over and over again whilst in that dark, 'Jacob, why did you not give me the death I deserved?'

It has been said many times, there is no existence of time in our world. Let me tell you, the dark was a life sentence. Only when the dark became lighter, still a low level, the figure stood in front of me. He had been allowed to descend from level one. 'You gave yourself up willingly. I felt in that moment your guilt and remorse; it became automatic to offer my arm. Anoku,' he said, 'you are not like the others. You learnt forgiveness before your return, you also learnt forgiveness before I.' Then he was no longer there.

Not until many challenges and level five did we greet each other again. Respect for each other, for respect and love is in our world. (Anoku was one of three who killed Jacob's wife when they lived on another world.) There is a saying in your world: one soul, many lives. Choice is always there. A soul may enter a body and return when that body dies; the soul may remain, or return again and again to whichever world. We will use earth as an example. One soul may return and return, another soul may return to different worlds, a soul may return again and again.

You are all intelligent people, it does not take much understanding. If you return, you return with a blank canvas. To return knowing of a previous life would be like walking through treacle. To try and pick up strands of a previous life would be unkind. On our world, you know of each life – that is preparation, great knowledge, great learning of each life.

There are those on our world who would never enter a body. Put a name on them if you wish, call them angels, helpers of the source. So, each time you return, you know of each life because the essence of that life remains.

Where is that home? The great facet? It is not coincidence those that cross your path have crossed your path before. The facet is great and each family is great, for those strands hold us all together. So, do we understand when someone crosses your path and you feel you knew them from before? The subconscious recognises that strand. So for all of you, have no fear, the essence of each life remains. The contract is your choice. There are those you wish to meet and those you don't respect. Again, it is always a choice, and love is always present.

I, Anoku, and Jacob have climbed great mountains to become pure and full of love. Your mountains will be small hilltops only. For one of you who sits today, the ground is level and the wind blows and that kite flies high in the wind.

A new energy will join on our next visit. I will not say this is my last visit, I leave that gateway open. Let it be known the privilege to serve – not only to serve, for I have gained great knowledge from you. Mankind, unforeseen knowledge, changes the landscape of your earth. Knowledge in the wrong hands has great danger. Knowledge also brings great rewards but can also be man's downfall. Man has so much to learn; transparency will come.

My blessings from the great source, the essence of you all. That door will remain open, if I am granted.

Au revoir, my friends.

03-06-2022   STELLA

Hello, everybody, please call me Stella.

I was born in a little town – Kalisz, Poland, was it my misfortune to be a Jew? I make no apologies for my tale. Forgiveness in our world, but never to forget! It was an idyllic life, Pa was a bookkeeper; Ma, self-taught, a talented seamstress; and I was studying to become a nurse.

The upheaval was fast, swift and I must underline the word brutal. They called themselves the 'master race', the Jews the scum of the earth. They would treat their guard dogs better than the Jews. I have chosen the year 1941; that was the year of my return home to the world of spirit, where my family were at rest awaiting my return. Does this story require telling, you may ask? It is through my eyes and my eyes only. Twenty minutes to midnight, the screeching of lorries, the thundering knock on the door. Not to answer quick enough, the doors torn off their hinges. In no time at all, in the clothes that we wore and barefoot, segregated males, females, and children. I was torn from my family and put into a lorry with young females only.

So our journey began, the screams lay in the distance. Gunshots rang out into the night sky. Soon it was daylight and one by one we departed the lorry. The smell of rotting flesh filled the nostrils, bodies lying on the edge of the road. In time the air became pure, the fields green and the fields were many. As the lorries screeched to a halt once more, it was my time to depart.

SOUL RESCUE FROM SUNRISE

I stood on the gravel in awe of the home before me. My eyes had never set upon such a grand dwelling. Staff lined up, soldiers, many guard dogs patrolling – yes, German shepherds and Dobermans, what else? Orders barked out, a maid stepped out and handled me roughly. As I was led inside, the floor was like a chess board, a grand staircase, orders barked out. 'Scrub her well, fine clothes only.'

I was marched up the stairs and stripped. My mind was racing 110%, my body shaking with fear. We were alone, and the maid apologised. 'I am a Jew also,' she stated. 'Do not ask, just obey to stay alive.' I was covered in powder. 'I am not an animal,' I said. Again she replied, 'Do not ask.' Washed and scrubbed, my hair cut short, no curls remained. Fine clothes did not stop the flood of tears, my cheeks were raw. 'You have to pull yourself together,' the maid said, 'or you will not last the night.'

How the hours ticked by, how the body ached and was numb. Then he entered, to me he was old, for I was eighteen years old, what did I know? He was a high-ranking officer, that is the only information I will give you. It would be wrong to name him, because to this day his children and their children's children, good honest families who have achieved in different countries live on. He was striking in looks, in his mid-thirties, and to his credit he was not like the others below him. All I could think about was my family. The first words out of my mouth, 'What of my family?' His reply: 'They are in separate camps, they are well looked after, do not ask again.'

I was eighteen years old and naive to the demands of the body. Soon I was to learn that I was to be spared because of my beauty, as were the other females. There were eighteen of us altogether.

I was never to set eyes on them again. I was never to set eyes on my family until 1941, October 6th. I was quick to learn, to become a skilled actress, a skilled actress in the bedroom, quick to learn his desires, on how to please his sexual needs. He was never brutal and those below had orders to respect me in a life of torment.

It was only at mealtimes a glimmer of joy, all the servants ate in the kitchen, and to me the kitchen was grand on a vast scale. My life was four walls, a bathroom, a bedroom, and servant's quarters; no other part of that vast home was I allowed. Grand trappings off the back of the Jewish community. At mealtimes there was always two guards to limit the conversation. No outside news; that home was our world and that home only. The only respite for me was when the officer was called away for days on end. In time I began to regret his absence, for on his return he was more demanding. Oh, how I tried and tried to wash away the filth inside of me.

Although the presence of guards, news would filter through, the maid and I became friends and to my horror, she spoke of mass killings and death camps. We all asked the same question: 'Are our families alive? Will we see them again?' I do not respect the German race; one is not superior to others. 'We are your masters,' they would say. The female servants were treated the same as I, raped continuously, with orders never to be brutal. The staff had purpose, and they knew the layout of this vast home. The time would come when maids were sent to clinics to rid the inferior disease growing inside them, for they could not dilute the German strain.

August 1941, I was to become pregnant, and I knew the fate of my child, my child was going to die with me. The bed where I was to become a skilled actress was to become my saviour. The officer, grandness from other quarters, one four-poster bed, silk curtains embroidered and a pull string rope. I chose my time, I did not let on that I was pregnant. Upon his absence, doing his duty, splendid furniture to scale, to tie that noose was so easy and that leap, the exit, so, so quick. There is so much that I could have said, which would alarm those present, so I scrimp on so many details.

It was dark for a short time, then I awoke looking up at the sky and clouds, so pale in colour. A sky I had not seen the like, the clouds of many colours as they drifted over. I looked around, I was in a small room with white walls, and the floor was white. A simple bed with white sheets. As I lay there, I lay mesmerised by the beautiful sky, a tiny voice spoke out. 'Mama, we are home.' My child perfectly formed, 'Annabella,' I cried.

The time was short, as the walls dispersed all around, green fields surrounded us. We walked barefoot, hand-in-hand, aimlessly across the fields. There was my home, everything was familiar, there was Ma and Pa. 'You are home Stella with your beautiful child. Do not look back,' they said. 'Do not revisit the atrocities, never return, forgive but do not forget.' On that journey on the back of the lorry, little did I know that those souls who lined those streets were the lucky ones, for they no longer suffered, they were home.

There are those on earth to this present day that hate fills their bones. Few in numbers but hate fills their veins. Only upon their return to the world of spirit will that hate be deceased. The scar will remain with the Jewish community, for the scars are past on to their children and grandchildren never to forget the heroics of their forefathers.

The next entry to your little circle will be a lot lighter. I put forward a shepherd to look after the flock, and you are the flock, my friends. My shepherd, the greatest Jew on earth.

Forgive those who cross you on earth, and the crossing will be smooth. The golden staff will remain, draw that golden staff on the wooden heart and put my name below therefore I shall never forget those of this day.

Farewell.

08-07-2022   MESSENGER

Greetings, I am one of many Messengers.

It has been discussed many times before, the eradication of disease in your world. Let us talk of pioneering surgery, many professors of note, and medical scientists. There are many that return to your world, for the good of your world, for the well-being of the human race. Those professors work closely, as we speak, in those laboratories. Structures for nerve end damage, thought of as damage beyond repair, breakthrough will bring those with paralysed limbs 70% of normal use, to improve the quality of life vastly.

Also, as we speak, there is a material being formulated to replace archaic metal and to replace bone in the human structure. Material so flexible and so hard wearing to see out a human lifetime. No need for replacements once inserted, it is so flexible it can work better than nature provides.

Yes, robots are the future generation for operations, and also laser. Let it be known, a surgeon will always stand by, for machines can break down. Procedures must be put in place, hence the longevity of the human body. Time will come when tumours will be removed, that will scarcely affect the workings of the human, and scar tissue heals at a far, far faster rate.

Breakthrough after breakthrough, you do not have to be a professor for one to work closely with. We are going to give you examples: a local farmer, why not be a local farmer? Chosen with an open mind, for organic farming. Organic is the future, pesticides are harmful to the environment. Animals that go to slaughter, traces of pesticides not totally eradicated, and they find their way into the human chain. A young man, a farmer harvesting crops, a major breakdown on the machinery while attempting to repair. The severing of a limb and the loss of blood, he returns to our world. A young farmer with an open mind, he works closely from farm to farm, with thoughts put into the minds of others.

Examples we give: a teacher in education, now in our world, was thought to be off the wall in your world. Radical ideas in teaching, he also goes from school to school to search out teachers to work with. Spirituality will become the norm in all schools, but not how you think.

Many views, many cultures, no segregation, no prejudice. Pupils will be taught there is life after life on earth. Yes, it will take time, but this will become the norm – spirituality on earth will blossom. Many, many countries will learn of the great playground where the children ride bareback on the wild animals. Books will be written, and the time will come when infants will read those books. It will be the beginning of worlds coming together.

Hate dispersing, the beginning of greed dispersing. What you see all over your world, where one country dictates and brutalises the innocent... slowly but surely, this will be eradicated.

Which do you say is important? Do you humans have greater importance than animals, insects, and nature? All are linked together; not one is more important than the other. For one to be eradicated without rebirth, slowly but surely the top of the chain would crumble and decay. So much put into place in our world. There are those of you that belong to this little gathering who choose to return and work closely with another, but be told, you can return at any time. The mind of those that return is so, so pure it can penetrate the energy thought patterns of the human brain. In layman's terms, it's easy to step into that elevator and you are home. That elevator remains, to step in and press return and you are back with the chosen one, with whom to work. For us, it is thought and we are there. All those that return from their human life, this becomes the norm.

This is a small insight into the future. The time will come when the dark will not penetrate, subdued for all eternity. To wither and die, only then will all targets be met – a world of peace, tranquillity, and love.

Messenger bidding farewell.

19-08-2022   MESSENGER

Greetings, it is I, Messenger.

The channel, releasement of the trapped souls, are those of the Korean War. Each pay their respects in their own way. Those stand in prayer, their hands pressed firmly together as one. There are those that salute, and those that stand and bow their heads. The first one comes with a sword and lays that sword across the sword already on the Beechwood heart in the centre of your circle, and that forms the cross of peace. As they pass over into our world, the peace overwhelms them and their troubled souls. They come in one behind the other, respect for those that have fallen, and respect for their brothers they have fought alongside from both camps.

When you think of all those countries in your world at war, picture the cross of swords as you ask for peace. Also ask for those that have fallen to return to our world so the releasement can be complete.

As we move on, the advanced technologies in your world, every changing day, old becomes new. Let us talk on that crude word you use – robots. Countries of your world where there is the technology, you have the small screen for entertainment; this has become the norm. Let me tell you, so it will become so with the robots; they will become the norm. Those countries that have the technologies, their uses will be vast. Those that limit their uses, they want companionship and they may choose male or female. It has been said that they will have skin that will feel like human skin, it will breathe and sweat. You may choose one that looks young, one that you would call mature, or one that is old – whatever suits the individual. There will be those that choose them to do the household chores, they will vacuum, iron, and others will keep dates to remind of appointments where the mind is vague. Also keeping tabs on their medication. One thing they will all have, and there will be no choice in this matter, there will be a built-in alarm to protect. Laws will be written: if an intruder comes into the house, they can defend. The owner of the household will be free of all charges, for it is law.

What you call the armed forces, there will be robots, again in their masses. To protect human life, your policing, they will travel in pairs – one human and one robot. Crime will fall at a fast rate, for where they defend and a human loses his life, no crime is committed. This in itself reduces crime. Each robot, no matter what the disguise, male or female, there will be a built-in alarm. Every martial art you wish to mention, the ultimate bodyguard, the ultimate fighting machine. Different classes built for the purpose. Those in the home, as technology develops, the old model traded in for the new with a financial difference to make up. Just as those square boxes (cars) you use for transport, to exchange one for another. Each robot programmed to voice command; they read the voice patterns, they are unique to each individual. They will only answer to those they are programmed to. You may think this is a flaw to explore, but they are tamper-proof. When the time comes for them to be exchanged, you can guess what I am going to say. They are recycled, for that is the way of your world.

Now let us move on again, to matters far, far more important. What is more important on your world than human life? Countries on your world, where there is drought, famine, and disease. No matter what you say, help is there. The greed of some countries in your world, they do nothing. This will change where there is poor leadership. If through greed, culturally developed countries will come together as one. They will put sanctions on other countries to act; they will have no choice. Drains will be built, water will flow to parched lands where soil will become fertile again. Crops will grow, medications will come by air, by oceans and land, diseases eradicated. For the levelling up of your world is necessary.

So much talk on your world of the Golden Age. How does this come about when your earth is not balanced? Is it right, when one country flourishes and another does not? There are those that die before their time. Agonising deaths, malnourished and riddled with disease. Levelling up must come to your world. So much talk of ascension, and yet we hear the chosen few again. This is wrong. There is a small saying on your world – think back and you will know where this saying is from: 'All for one and one for all.' A united world, where one is no better than the other. Yes, there will always be leaders, ones who are fair to all and not just to those who are rich and those with power. Oh, how governments in your world will change. Cultures will change only through the coming together of cultures in partnership, and their children educated by both parents on both cultures.

They will grow and partner other cultures, and they will educate and so on and so on. It will go on until prejudice does no longer exist. So much talk on the Golden Age, as though it is light years away. So much preparation, so many backward steps. Rest assured, my friends, there will be a levelling up of all countries. The suffering of the human will only come from one who commits crime on the other. That will be the last hurdle on your world. You have a mountain you call Everest. You all sit at the bottom of Everest. Only when you reach the summit will the Golden Age arrive.

My time with you this day is complete, so to let others talk of their journey when you next come together. At that time, when those that come with their journey are complete, I Messenger will return. The knowledge of your world future, past, and present, requires to be spoken. Do not ever dismiss the past, for the past makes each individual, as does the present.

Again, Lady Ann, you have choice. All of you that sit can think of that sword that lies across the other. You may place a sword across the wooden heart in the centre of your table. A little sneak into your future: you will require a bigger heart! There are those that would be honoured to have their place upon the heart. No matter how many hearts you may have, and when this little circle does not exist, when that time comes we ask of those that remain, if only one, to burn those hearts together and scatter those ashes to the winds of those great oceans. That is the wish of our world, they will remain in those winds and those oceans for eternity.

It is my privilege to be with you and know that I am chosen to return again and again.

Farewell.

02-09-2022   PEGGY Re: LOU

Hello, I am Peggy, but call me Lou.

I was born and reared Newquay, Wales. My parents purchased a failing convenience store, but within five years it was a thriving business. There was living accommodation above the store, which my parents let out to a trusted friend. He was an English teacher, and they purchased a two-bedroomed cottage on the edge of the countryside.

Soon after, I was born, christened Peggy Louise. My dad wasn't to get his way. He said to my mom, 'As she grows up, her friends will call her Peg.' So I was Louise (Lou). On working days I would spend my time above the store, where mom would pop in now and then to check on me. As the years continued, I became a very shy, quiet child. I didn't make friends, my friend was always a book. I would lose myself in the children's stories.

I was considered a bright child, my school reports were always glowing – except for one department. 'Peggy,' teachers would say, 'she is very quiet, she does not mix.' My results were always excellent, my favourite subjects History and Science. Everything came easy to me – English, maths, geography. My 'O' levels easy, and then to progress to 'A' levels. At school I was thought of as a book swot, more interested in what was in a book than friends around me.

I was seventeen years old when my life was to change dramatically. An older man came into my life. He made me feel alive. He was the only person to ever take any interest in me besides my parents. To the horror of my mom and dad, I was seventeen years old and expecting a baby. The father disappeared overnight, never to be seen again.

Motherhood was very, very difficult for me. It was decided that mom would look after Walter, and I would work in the store with dad. This in itself became a double blessing – a blessing for me, as mom became Walter's mom. This gave me the escape and the other blessing, I was to learn all about the business. I was to serve the customers, order stock, and keep the accounts. I would hear customers say, 'Isn't Lou quiet, it's like pulling teeth trying to have a conversation with her.' Dad used to laugh it off. How I used to wish I was like mom and dad, they were very outgoing and social. Where did I fit in? I was the complete opposite, to busy myself in a book to stop myself thinking that way.

Walter was now five years old. I remember his party so well. Parents would bring round their children and I would sit in the corner. Mom entertained them all. A milestone in Walter's life. A milestone in my life; I sat in the corner, everyone joking and laughing. I was sitting there wishing the room would swallow me up.

Eventually when Walter was eight years old, I became more of a mother, as mom went back to work in the store. I spoke of a double blessing. As dad became ill, I was to run the store. My training beforehand would become a blessing to both mom and dad. Mom would stay at home to look after dad. She interviewed an assistant to work alongside me. Yes, she was very outgoing and very chatty, much to my relief. She would take the pressure off me when the customers would want to chat, as we were taught would bring them back again and again, that was the personal touch.

Dad's illness was short, pneumonia got the better of him. In time mom returned to work back in the store. Walter was now eleven years old, his grandad passed. I loved Walter but was never close to him. I wished I was more like my parents, but that wish backfired, for Walter was a mirror image of myself. Walter had hardly any friends, he was very shy, almost reserved. He did have one friend, Diane, from his early days at school. Walter was bullied, it was only when her family came into the neighbourhood – they were a feisty family (Diane and two brothers) – Diane would stick up for Walter against the bullies. Diane knew that the reputation of her brothers would back her all the way. So it went on through school days, hand-in-hand through the teenage years, Diane was his protector. Both were very bright, again, schooling came easy, but Walter had no ambition. Diane was the opposite, she went on to university.

Walter almost became a hermit, he refused to get out of bed in the morning, he had no interest in finding a job. They said it was clinical depression. He, too, would read into the early hours of the morning, then stay in bed until late afternoon. If Walter wasn't reading, he was writing to Diane. The guilt I felt inside of me as I could see so much of myself in Walter. I didn't like what I saw, his reluctance to find a job, a job his qualifications deserved. I had no choice but to bring him into the store to work. 'Young man,' I said, 'you have got to start paying your way, you can no longer live rent-free.' So Walter was paid a wage and joined the store.

Over ten years passed, and Walter knew all that I knew on running the store. Letters would come from Diane; he would only tell me bits and drabs. I knew she worked in law and lived in London. She had purchased a flat and was doing very well.

The profit in our shop started to decline. As small supermarkets were developed, we could not compete with those prices. We would pride ourselves with customer satisfaction, and the core of the customers stayed loyal. The inevitable happened: we had to sell up the store and accommodation above. The last straw for myself was to see that little shop bulldozed to the ground. 'Development for social housing' they called it. The purpose in my life had gone, mom had joined dad, I'm sure they would be talking the hind legs off their family, whom they had joined.

I used to spend my days in the garden, how I loved the garden. On mom's passing, I transformed dad's vegetable patch. I planted roses of every sort, the ground was so fertile, how I loved roses.

Walter had now grown up into a man. Ironically, he was to work at the local supermarket, where he was snapped up for his expertise. He soon became the manager, again to his reluctance, the 'head man'. To interview recruits, for his wisdom on every department none could better. There were times he chose to work nights and spend his days lost in a book.

On that fateful day, it was the beginning of the end. I had a fall, causing bruising of my side, an X-ray revealed cracked ribs but that was not all. Also a mass had been found that needed investigating. On breaking the news to me, I made a decision. Right or wrong, was I thinking of myself or was I thinking of Walter? I was not going to let him watch me shrivel and die in front of his eyes. It was still easy, and while I could still walk to the local chemist, you would call it a cocktail of drugs. Walter would find me, laying on my bed with a sealed envelope on my chest with his name on it.

The last thing I recall was numbness and darkness, then I awoke and it was light. It was a lightness I had never felt before – the dark burden that had been with me all of my life had gone. There was mom, dad, nan and grandad, who I did not know. As they wrapped their arms around me, they uttered, 'We understand, Walter will thrive. In time, you will be able to watch him flourish.'

Again, it was a double blessing – the relief I felt, and I like to think that my death brought Diane back into Walter's life. Diane returned after hearing the news. After the funeral, she wasted no time. 'Walter,' she said, 'now your mother is no longer there to look after you, I will be there.' 'I am a grown man,' said Walter. 'I enjoy my work, and you have your life which is very different to mine.' Diane had relationships, but none that had worked out; she had one love only. Having relationships that kept breaking down made her realise.

Diane poured her heart out. 'Walter, my life belongs with you.' She was to leave the law firm and sell her flat. She moved in with Walter, and lived her days in the cottage. She was to work in the local supermarket. She would not allow Walter to dwell.

Holidays became the norm, a favourite place was Lyme Regis. They first purchased a caravan and then a chalet. Money was not a problem. They are now both retired, and to this day back and forth they go. They spend the summer months in Lyme Regis and the winter months in the cottage – the home that was always my home and also Walter's. They don't have children; they have made their wills, and the cottage will go to charity.

The purpose of my visit: it was my wish to be like my parents, Walter was like me, which I didn't like. There are parts of us that we wish to change. From our world, you see things so differently. Accept what you are and who you are; above all, be kind to yourself. I try to let you know how wrong my thinking was throughout my time. Only in this world is there clarity, and it is never too late to change.

As my energy fades, I see a new energy – a man with a full headdress of feathers. He will make his presence known at your next gathering.

Goodbye.

16-09-2022 WATER RUNS DEEP

Greetings, my people, Water Runs Deep greets you all.

First, to acknowledge all those present and the essence of those that are not. Water Runs Deep is known to Master Peter. I am not alone, for my daughter, Feather in Wind is with me.

Greetings, Feather in Wind here to pay my respects and acknowledge all those who are present and the essence of those who are not. I am one of a few, you would call a spirit guide. Let me be clear for all of you, your guides from all sources that cater for all your needs are there for your arrival onto this earth. They are with you until you depart and return home to be with your ancestors. If it be one moon or many moons, it matters not. To me it is a privilege to observe my father speaking with you. I now merge to my rightful place, behind my father's energy.

First, Lady Ann, let me be clear, my headdress, shall we put it in simple terms? If you were to attend a special ceremony, you may wear special headgear. The status you bestow on me, know that I am not a chief; I am a teacher of herbs and potions. You know of the medicine man, a status befitting I hold, I sit with the elders and, yes, to know my place, as we all do.

It is my wish for all of you to tread the path of cinder and ash, the remains of the fire, a pure path cleansed, that is my wish. Simple people, my people are the

Cherokee, to work with the children for the knowledge of the trees that grow and the animals that walk this land. There is one fine bird that freely gives it feathers, meat, sinew, and bone. The sinews to tie together the skins, the bone so soft to crush with the leaves of the great trees, and the fruit they bear to grind together.

My great daughter, Feather in Wind, has wisdom so advanced for her time. Her mentor, Grey Cloud, Master Gary, his presence with you since you touched this earth. For the wisdom to teach and pass on that knowledge is an honour.

The path of cinder and ash, Master Gary, it is hard stone you have travelled on your pathway but it is lined with the great feathers of the great bird that gives for our people. This bird does not soar the great skies, for the turkey sustains our life.

Young braves learn to hunt at a teaching school – the great bear that gives power and wisdom; the deer that runs free; and the small game. All those teachers have status. Young squaws, as simple as it may seem, have to be taught to light a fire, to bind the skins, to kill small animals. And the boys to hunt to become a man, the task to bring back the turkey and then the deer. Only when the bear is slain are they really worthy of becoming a man. All know their place, for the cycle has to be complete for the survival of our people.

You pray to the one God; we pray to the winds, to the great waters, the moon, the sun, and the stars that talk. The greatest gift is to look into the flames of the fire and the smoke, the great spirit wisdom, proud, proud people. No decision is ever made without acknowledging the great spirit. We live our life and obey the spirit of the counsel; that is our rule, and that rule must be obeyed.

On this day, a day of great reckoning in our world, you lay the wooden heart where many leave their mark. I say to you all, each of you have your own heart – it may be handmade, it matters not. On that heart, place the names of those close to you. Place the names on that path of cinder and ash for their path to be pure and cleanse the negativity from their souls. This is a great gift for you all, for no greater gift can you give than to purify the soul. I place my hands, one by one, on the brow of each of you. The blessings of the spirit be with you. Feel that light pressure on the brow of you all. With those names on that heart and the pure pathway, draw around your own hands and colour them in colours that come to mind. It matters not what colour they are or how many colours. Place your hands on them, and then you can give healing by thought or by touch. These are great gifts you are all worthy of.

My gift, the pipe of peace, to bring together all nations that are at war. A gift from my great daughter, the feather of the turkey to place on a new wooden heart at the centre of your table. Names will come in, and each to be written in the colour they request. Lady Ann, I ask of you to think of the one who opened this channel and the one who he cannot be separated from (Mark and Adele). Those names are to be written in gold at the head of the heart. They will be embroidered in the great book in the great library. You will find our people in the great library. Each culture will read in their own way. I sit in that great library, where the flame burns bright, and the smoke will instruct, as it did this day, as the flame becomes a flicker.

The souls continue to pass, our people are not amongst them; our ways for the soul are different, there is no entrapment. Simple people who live their lives and spirit communication is second nature. I ask this one thing before the flame dies: make your heart simple. All those guides that work with Master Peter, work simple. As those who are wise, the wise guides fit. Let it be known, Lady Ann, your guides are from the higher realms.

I do not forget those that sit, the pink ray nurtures, great honours, Lady Pat. Lady Elsie, a golden key that opens doors. What would life be if there was only one chapter? Lady Anita, the gifts you have to heal the ground you walk on, also other worlds. Master Gary, the stone covered with the feathers of the turkey, you have that knowledge to pick out that wisdom from the stone.

The smoke forms the circle, blessings to you all, my people. I speak for my daughter; her blessings also as the flame dies.

Farewell.

19-09-2022 CISSY, JANICE

Hello, everyone, it is only polite to acknowledge all that assemble here today. The energy that you create allows us to be with you. With respect, I shall work with names that we are christened with as we touch this earth, although they were shortened for the lifetime endured. I am Cissy, known as Ciss.

It is my hope that a little knowledge comes your way. As a parent we can become unaware of the adverse effect we have on our children or child. I shall speak as I viewed through my eyes. My daughter Janice is here this day; she will view through her eyes. Ah yes, you will see a difference that I could not see.

My husband Robert, who was Bob, my eldest daughter Angelina, known as Ange, and Janice was Jan. Two daughters so very different. Robert was so disappointed when Jan was born, he so wanted a son. To say he settled for second best is not quite correct, but it will be fit for what I say. Angelina was a tomboy who always mixed with the boys from a very early age and played footie with her dad and the boys. Cricket also they loved to play.

The one sport the girls did have in common was tennis. Angelina would beat Janice every time, and so she would play against the boys. Some games she would win and some she would lose. Those losses made her more determined, as she didn't like to lose.

Jan was a girlie girl, and Bob was all for Ange. I would say to him spend more time with Jan. I was very concerned about this over the years, but he would say, 'You can only do girlie things with Jan.'

When they became teenagers and old enough to take an interest in boys, Jan would bring home a boy, or should I say, young man. Bob would say to me, 'Ange never brings a boy home.' As a mom, I had a little word with her and she said, 'I will bring a boy home, mom, no problem.' 'A boyfriend?' I said. 'Yes, no problem.'

Bob was over the moon; I was not convinced, neither was Jan. As a mom you notice things, often a dad can be oblivious. Not only did Ange dress differently, Jan would go to nightclubs with the girls and Ange would go to other clubs. One young man, Tom, became a regular with Jan, going steady, we would say.

Again Bob would question. Ange had such a close bond with her dad. 'Mom,' she said, 'I'm going to bring my friend home and introduce her to dad, he will understand,' she said.

That night, she brought home her friend – a night I will never forget! Bob exploded. I have never seen such rage in all our married years. 'Pack your bags and leave, and never return!' Those words I took to my grave. In a strange way, I thought Jan would then benefit from her dad, but this was not to be and the years rolled by. Jan was married with two sons. I was so pleased, for her life was good. Tom was a good husband, dad, and son-in-law; you could wish for no better. There were times Tom and Bob would play golf together, a bond there.

I used to think to myself, Jan is getting that love from Tom, the close bond she did not get from her dad. My mind never strayed from not knowing where Ange was. Was she happy? Secrets in a family which are kept locked close into one's heart. Although my girls were so different, they were always close. Without my knowledge, that bond remained, a secret kept from their mom. Jan also kept the secret from her husband and sons. She would keep Ange updated on family affairs.

One day Bob fell, he would brush it all off. 'I lost my balance, that is all,' he would say. He was fit and we thought healthy, there were no outward signs otherwise. Another fall and another one. Reluctantly an appointment with the GP. A scan revealed a tumour that lay behind the eyes. We went back and forth, medical opinions. To operate would be far too dangerous.

While he still had his senses, 'Cissy,' he said. 'Ciss, don't let me suffer. Leave the drugs out, I will take them, it is my choice.' Each time I refused, I hid them and he would search and search. When the time drew near, morphine dulled his pain but also his senses. Just the three of us were allowed at the bedside. At times he was conscious, he was aware, only then did the secret come out.

Jan blurted out, 'Ange should be here!' 'No,' he would shout, or try to shout. 'Jan,' I replied, 'we don't know where she is.' 'I do,' she replied. 'She is here in the waiting room.' A reaction from Bob caused him to become unconscious. 'Jan,' I said, 'stay with dad and hold his hand tight.'

I had no time to wait for the lift, I rushed down flights of stairs. I threw my arms around my daughter as the tears flowed. Ange sat there quietly, hands wrapped around her dad's and Jan's. I held his other hand and spoke gently to him. 'Ange is here,' I said. 'Squeeze my hand to let me know you can hear me.' The response was immediate. The tears flowed again from Ange; not a single tear left Jan's eyes.

All my friends call me Ciss, my friends, goodbye from Ciss.

JANICE

Hello, Janice here, now let us be a little more upbeat, shall we? Mom spoke of how she always saw life. Ange, how dad worshiped her. 'Yes,' mom would say, 'what about Jan?' My view was very different, mom was so oblivious of the pain. Don't let me drag you down, the pain I felt. I was so close to mom and yet she couldn't see I loved dad, and yet I didn't have a dad in the sense of the word.

Mom knew from the early days that Ange was gay, did it matter? Not to us; happiness is all that counts. My life was full, two-thirds. Mom could only see Tom, a loving husband, and two loving children. Mom could see life was good, and it was good. Ange was gone for so many years of mom's life. Although I was close to mom, did I feel guilty? NO!

Ange made me swear, that's not to say I never felt a moment's guilt. Why feel guilt that can only drag you down? That is what mom did, she could never see the hurt that I hid so well, so desperate to be loved by dad. That was one of mom's misgivings, where she was unaware, and dad was unaware also. Dad was also oblivious to the fact that I kept in touch with Ange. I kept her informed of everything going on in the family.

Tom was not happy when he found out, but he waited for the grieving process before he spoke. Was it wrong of me, I didn't grieve? Yes, I loved dad, but I was cold, cold inside. That one part of me the fire could not reach. Other than that, my life was good.

My friends, do not carry guilt, do not carry the burden. Look at the riches in your life. If you have children, they are blessings however they turn out. If you do not have children, then know your friends are blessings also.

Tom allowed for grieving when there was no need. 'You kept a secret from me,' he said. 'We have always been honest with one another.' It was so hard to make him understand. I swore to Ange, and I didn't want to break that trust. It was hard for him to take in. I think it chipped at his ego. It healed in time, and I assured him we are honest and the trust is always there.

Now in our world, mom, dad, and I unite, we look through the same eyes. Mom can see the mistake she made, and dad also. I, my friends, am crystal clear, am I not? Was I wrong to feel no guilt? Now I view an emotion that was stripped away inside from that cold part of me. My friends, if there is a part of you that you need to heal before you return, it is my wish to ask of you to heal that part.

Ange does not have long, my friends, before she returns home. The tough cookie that cried in floods of tears as she held mine and dad's hand. I was always thought of as the soft one, so we really see when we view through our own eyes.

My friends, and I call you that respectfully, Lady Ann, I ask of you, Cissy opened and I will close. This is not sexist; it is an honour to have our names on your wooden heart of peace, we ask these names to go under the name of Adele. The heart of peace has many, many avenues, for peace comes in many forms. Don't just think of those at war. There is an emotional hurt, mental and emotional happiness, peace comes in so many, many forms.

My mother's colour was very much the shade of the roses you have in your little room, Lady Ann (magenta). My colour, I wish for part yellow and part white, a beautiful flower, so simple. As a child I would pull the petals off one by one and leave the yellow centre, the stem, so so strong. The strength of that stem goes to you all.

Goodbye, my friends.

(The colours refer to the names that are to be written on the wooden heart in the centre of the table where we sit in our circle.)

14-10-2022   ANGELINA

Hello Angelina here, it was so easy for me to return, mom spoke so highly of you all. Not twenty-four hours had passed on your last meeting until my return. Janice held my hand for this return but there was no need, for the earth's energies have such a great pull at this moment in time. My passing was so sweet and gentle, to retire early in my old age, sleep was never a problem.

I awoke standing in the doorway of our home, with dad standing in front of me. 'You're home, lass,' he said. 'You're home.' So strange yet so familiar. Mom and Janice stood behind with beaming smiles. Dad got down on one knee. 'Forgive me, lass,' he said. 'The narrow-mindedness no longer exists, just love that has no bounds.' Those days are so vivid in my mind, to bring my girlfriend home and for him to explode.

Ostracized, to be frank. My girlfriend was adamant she would not leave the town she loved, she would not leave her job. We parted on good terms as I waved goodbye to Glamorgan. My first pitstop was Nantwich, to book into a B&B for two nights to gather my thoughts. I tossed a coin – a lucky coin, I always thought. An old penny: heads for North, tails for South. Heads it was, so me and Bertie (that's what I called my car) we travelled North to Manchester. I had shopped there many times before.

Wrexham was dad's football team – a long way from Glamorgan. We had travelled there many times by car, other times there was a coachload. It is surprising when you are upset and so desperate what little you travel with. I crammed my possessions into a suitcase and left a wardrobe of clothes behind. I took my valued possessions and a few clothes, birthday cards, handwritten and those made with cheap paper and coloured with crayons. I took the football that dad always said was a match ball from those days at Wrexham. There was no proof, but that's what he always claimed.

That football followed me to my grave. Although I was always popular, as time goes by and those wither and die one by one, there was just one at my funeral. A friend, a born Scouser, and that was to eventually become my home – Liverpool. My Welsh accent and their accent, we both strained to understand each other at times.

I had a brief stop at Manchester but it did not fit. Liverpool fitted like a glove, such friendly people, and there my new journey began. To wipe the slate clean, discover my true self. What work was I good at? I loved sport, sport of all sorts. My name went down at the local job centre, a brief interview. Would you believe, a vacancy came through at a sports shop! I was what you would call a glorified saleswoman. But what I didn't know, and to work with the men, so so refreshing.

The men and lads, I would say to them, 'What studs do you require?' for their football boots. They would look at me in astonishment. The cricketers: 'What type of bat do you require? Are you left-handed or right? Do you want the dense wood or the soft wood?'

Those that worked with me would pick my brains. It was not long before promotion came. I also had a head for figures and promotion came again. I was to work in the office, but it became stale. I took a wage cut to go back onto the shop floor, the shop floor, that's where I belonged.

I continued to support Liverpool and, yes, lowly Wrexham, I would still watch them, I would think of dad and look at my football, my tears would flow. Janice would always keep me up to date. My name was never allowed to be mentioned. Little did dad and mom know Janice and I had shopping days in Manchester. There were times we would book into a hotel and dine out. Janice would say to me, 'You are so uncouth.' I drank out of a pint glass; her tipple was wine. She would easily get drunk, and oh, how she would giggle such happy days and happy nights to share.

My girlfriends came and went, the one true one was Angela – a blessing, a ring on one another's fingers. That day so vivid, it was July 1st – it was our fifteen-year anniversary. Just five short days later, that morning she was hard to wake, a stroke, she was barely alive. A simple wish, 'Those rings are precious,' Angela said. 'Whoever goes first, always wear that ring.'

On the return home, those rings tied together with red ribbon and placed at the base of the feet inside the coffin. The soul leaves the body from the soles of the feet; the fire welds them together for all eternity. Upon my return, Mom, Dad, Janice, and Angela were there. Dad went down on one knee and held out his hand,

and there were the rings. Angela came forward, as dad untied the ribbon and placed a ring on each of our fingers. 'I understand the love you share for each other,' dad said.

Lessons I have learnt: if there are those of you that sit this day and you have banished loved ones, where drifts have come along and never returned on the tides of the sea, fear not. For all will come together, for the tides of the sea bring driftwood, driftwood to come together as a jigsaw. Where there is a parting, each is a driftwood. I was a driftwood and dad was a driftwood. Upon my return, he placed that driftwood on the beach. I did not understand as they came together, it was only as I was standing in the doorway of our home did I understand.

I loved our town, although I was a Welsh girl, I also became a Scouser. My second home, such friendly people, a bond. Master Gary, it is my wish for you to place my dad's football below our names on the wooden heart of peace. It was a little heavier than those balls of today. The football, the colour of your choice, dad gives his stamp of approval.

Lady Ann, on the heart of peace under the name of Mark, the names of Goddess Aqua and your name Ann, both in gold. Abraham, Jacob, and Samuel, those names the colour of your choice, but they must be colours of the rainbow. Finally, my name in purple; some may say violet, again your choice. I will answer the subconscious mind of Master Peter, his mind just said, 'Why not red for Liverpool?' I chose purple, for that was my dad's favourite colour. The wreath that was placed upon his coffin was that colour, with the word DAD in the centre with white carnations.

The photo of that wreath was one of the possessions in my suitcase. I have Bib to thank for organising my funeral. Bridget her name, how she hated it; Bib she was known. A loyal friend for over twenty years. I was eighty-seven years, six months, and seven days. I was not aware of my journey home, as that driftwood joined together. It was only when dad appeared, I knew a serenity, a love so beautiful. Within two years, I know Bib will join us, there is plenty of room at the inn.

My beautiful souls, I speak of you all. The soul shines so bright; it dims a little when you close down. Be assured, where there is driftwood on this earth, it will come together. It will become one upon your return, and the return is where your home lies. It is where your soul is at peace. As those souls return, the importance of the colours of the rainbow. They each choose their colour of choice, as that colour eases their passing into our world.

Although it is easy for me to stay, there is so much beauty and love in our home. Return I may one day, if I do return, my wish is to have children. I would also like to be dainty and drink a glass of wine. My home town will be Liverpool, and my children will live and breathe Liverpool FC.

A strange, strange feeling, for the energies fade and the great magnet pulls. The privilege is so great for me to speak with you all. Master Gary, as the energies fade, as they are fresh in your mind, they will go on the heart of peace. Put your name in the colour of your choice, in the centre of the football. There is a jumble going on, for the energies fade so quickly.

Goodbye, gentle souls.

GLASTONBURY CALLING

Glastonbury, the most famous town in Somerset. It is believed to be a site of pre-Christian worship – a magical, mystical place, where the ruins of a medieval church still stand at the top of the Tor. The Tor being the highest of hills in Glastonbury. Lore has it that Jesus, as a boy, travelled to Glastonbury with his uncle, Joseph of Arimathea. Following Jesus' crucifixion, it is believed that Joseph travelled back to Glastonbury with the chalice Jesus used at his last supper and later by Joseph to catch Jesus' blood at his crucifixion. Upon his arrival, Joseph thrust his staff into the ground, and during the night his staff took root and grew into a thorn bush – the sacred Glastonbury Thorn. The chalice, lore states, it was buried at the foot of the Tor by Joseph of Arimathea upon his return.

My first call to Glastonbury – May 2004

Two weeks before my first visit to Glastonbury, whilst in trance one of my guides Simon came through and told me that I must go to Glastonbury. He said, 'There will be a lady, she will stand in front of a particular tree, you will know which tree because you will see her footprints in the grass, they will end where the sun casts a shadow on the ground.'

So, humbly trusting and following instructions, I arrived at the top of the Tor with a group of friends who belonged to my circle. I was aware of several different energies around, but no more than that. I was initially very disappointed.

My guide Simon then spoke to me. He told me to look up into the sky, pick out any cloud, and as I did so I instinctively began to follow it as it floated across the sky. I found myself walking away from the group and down the side of the Tor. I stopped and looked down into a field, where I noticed a gate in the far corner, two trees to the left, and one in the middle. I was drawn to the middle tree.

As I walked closer, I could hardly believe my eyes! The long grass had been trampled on, footprints leading straight from the gate to the middle tree. They stopped where the sun had cast the shadow of the tree, just as it had been prophesied two weeks earlier. Moving closer to the tree, I was unprepared for what was to follow. There were many monks in grey habits circling the tree. They all swung burning incense bowls as they walked. One of the monks stopped and turned towards me. He said, 'This is a quiet place only for prayer and meditation.' He emphasized, 'quiet meditation.' He then joined the circle of monks and they all disappeared. I was left totally bewildered.

My second call to Glastonbury – May 2006

My guide Simon came to me once again as I sat in my circle. He instructed me to return to Glastonbury, but this time with Anita. Anita was an earth healer who belonged to my circle. Simon informed me that Anita had been given a sword, symbolically a symbol of great power. The sword has the initials M and J interwoven on the hilt, intertwined with branches.

So again, I did as was asked and I arrived in Glastonbury along with Anita and two other friends. We climbed the Tor immediately, full of reverence for this sacred place. Simon had informed me that Anita would receive another gift from one of the monks. That is the only additional information I had been given. As we stood in front of the tree, Simon began speaking the words I was to relay to Anita. She was to take one step forward and strike the tree where the tree cast a shadow. To my amazement, before us stood four rows of monks, standing one behind the other. One monk stepped forward and Anita was told to hold out her hands. She was given a golden chalice, Anita was to take the chalice to the Chalice Well, to be placed in the well so the holy water could flow into it.

As we turned to leave the Tor, before me stood a monk in a red gown flowing to the ground. Embroidered on the gown was a magnificent gold cross. The monk waved to us to continue on with our journey to the Chalice Well. The chalice was duly placed on a plinth beneath the lion's head spout. I was informed by my guide that the water from Chalice Well would heal the souls of mankind, whosoever drank from it. We were all truly humbled by the whole experience.

My third call to Glastonbury – May 2007

Again Glastonbury called. My guides informed me that there was work to be done on top of the Tor – St Michael's Tower, within the arches. I was instructed by my guide Simon to take our friend Pat, who was also part of the circle, and her husband Ron, as their energies were needed. This time, whilst on top of the Tor, two soldiers appeared to me, each holding a spear, standing either side of the arched entrance. Anita was instructed to first strike the arch with her sword and then take her place in the centre of the Tor. Pat and Ron were to take their places one before and one behind her. The sword now had to be plunged through the middle flagstone in order to release negative, non-serving energies.

As the sword penetrated the earth, I saw before us a swirling vortex of pink light opening up and filling the whole space within the tower. Simultaneously, Anita was told to extend her left arm, hand facing down. A soldier stepped forward and presented Anita with a ring. It had a wide band like a man's wedding ring, it was rose gold in colour, and slightly battered. Again, the joined M and J letters and the branch design encircled the ring. I was told this ring was extremely important and as powerful as the sword but used for different purposes. This ring, I was informed, was to release trapped souls.

Once the ring had been presented to Anita, my guides instructed me to step forward, and I was given a staff – a staff, I was told, for leadership. I was informed that this belonged to Joseph of Arimathea. We were then instructed to make our way back down the Tor.

A short time later, we decided to revisit the Chalice Well, to walk around the garden and to try and begin to process exactly what had happened to us all that day!

We were in the gift shop, when a friend and member of the circle, Pat, was flicking through a book entitled *Evoking Mary Magdalene*. Pat asked me if the picture she was looking at in the book was in fact the chalice that Anita had been presented with upon our previous visit. To everyone's amazement, this beautiful print by Dante Gabrielle Rossetti, first painted in 1877, depicted Mary Magdalene holding the identical chalice which we had received from spirit some two years earlier!

My fourth call to Glastonbury – November 2014

Yet again I was instructed by my guides 'Sisters of Assisi' that Glastonbury was again calling. I was informed that two of our group were to go to the Tor in order to connect with the 'Sisters of Assisi', and instructions would follow. Over the next few weeks I was receiving messages constantly. I knew there was a very strong connection between Glastonbury and Italy, also between the Sisters of Assisi and The Knights Templar.

Again, we climbed up Wearyall Hill and we saw Joseph of Arimathea's desecrated tree. On the summit we could see the triangle of the Tor, the Abbey, and Wearyall Hill. At the bottom of the hill there were two Doberman dogs frolicking in the field with their owner. The largest of the two began bounding towards us. His owner called him furiously, but he obviously had no recall control. Afraid, I stood in front of my group trying to protect them, as their fear was palpable as the dog hurtled towards us. Suddenly, out of nowhere, a huge ram materialised before our very eyes. All members of the party witnessed this. He stood in front of us and bulked himself out. The Doberman also was startled and screeched to a halt three feet away. He quickly turned on his heels and ran back down the hill to his owner.

Startled by what we had experienced, I looked up and I saw Pat standing opposite me, and at her side stood a lady in a light grey hooded cloak. She held out a cloth, and I was told it was the cloth that had bathed Jesus' feet. I instructed Anita to put the ring she had been given into the cloth. Prior to our visit, members of the group had been given gifts by spirit, which we had been informed were to be relinquished at some point in time. We were instructed that they were to be placed on a large stone before us.

The ram stood firm throughout, as if our protector. He approached each and every one of us in turn, as if to greet us as individuals. When all the gifts had been relinquished, the lady in the grey hooded cloak made the sign of the cross. Amazingly, the ram dematerialized before our very eyes just as quickly as he had materialized. He just vanished as if into thin air! I knew he had done the job he had been assigned to do – our 'protector' – until our task had been completed.

The following day, which happened to be 9th November, Remembrance Sunday, we made our way to the tree at the bottom of the Tor. This was the tree for quiet prayer and meditation. After we had spent some time in quiet meditation, we formed a circle around the tree. I was given back the sword by spirit, which now had an additional golden hilt. Elsie, one of the group, was instructed to step forward to receive a golden key. A key to keep forever. Anita received a golden laurel crown; Pat, a silver cord, which she had previously received from the monk, like the hilt, it too was now a golden cord.

After all this had taken place, again a huge vortex appeared of swirling light energy of purple and pink hues. There was an intense powerful energy surrounding us all, I suddenly felt lightheaded and euphoric. I was told by my guide that the work we had completed was of great significance, it had released the monks and enabled them to work in the area of the triangle. I witnessed with my own eyes the hills around the Tor running bright red with blood!

Elsie had been instructed to turn the key. As she did so, the ground rumbled beneath our feet – a cleansing of the earth and its energy was taking place. 'The work can now begin,' I was informed. The only object we were not instructed to use during this ceremony was the rose gold ring. This, I was informed, was to be given to another individual for her work in soul rescue. In fact, it was the lady whose footprints I had seen and followed earlier in the grass at the foot of the Tor. Finally, I witnessed many, many monks standing shoulder to shoulder the breadth of the Tor, and with them stood Joseph of Arimathea.

This was an experience I feel very honoured to have been part of. An experience that will stay with me, and no doubt all members of the group, for the rest of our earthly lives.

Upon completion of our work, we returned to the bottom of the Tor, and as we reached the bottom we saw a large standing stone with three swans carved upon it. A symbol of transformation, we took this to represent the three points of the triangle... a job well done!

…And so the story continues… it is ongoing. I continue to channel spirit, I continue to meet once a fortnight in my closed trance circle, with my wife Ann and friends, chosen by spirit for this particular task – SOUL RESCUE. And to bear witness to souls who have been allowed to share their story with us, and thus allowing us to share their stories with you. I feel both privileged and humble to be in a position to share my story, supported by my wife and soulmate Ann, and her indomitable spirit of encouragement, without whom my story would have never been told. And I live in gratitude for the eternal loving guidance from my spiritual angels.

God bless you all,

                Pete Dawson

ACKNOWLEDGEMENTS

With gratitude to my beautiful wife and soulmate, Lady Ann, without whose perseverance and strength this book would have never been published.

With love and gratitude to everyone who sat many hours over many years, supporting the energies that facilitate the channelling of spirit. These include my beloved friends & family Elsie, Pat, Anita, Gary, Amanda and my wife Ann.

To Amanda, for many hours spent typing up my manuscripts ready for the publishing house.

To all of my Spirit guides, of which there are many, without whom there would be no book at all. Lastly, but most importantly, I have to thank all those souls who were willing to communicate through me in order to have their stories told.

SOUL RESCUE FROM SUNRISE

The wooden hearts & images as requested by spirit, to be placed in the centre of our table every time I channel spirit.

www.ingramcontent.com/pod-product-compliance
Lightning Source LLC
Chambersburg PA
CBHW061706180426
43192CB00055B/2829